# GENRE
# AND THE INVENTION
# OF THE WRITER

# GENRE
# AND THE INVENTION
# OF THE WRITER
*Reconsidering the Place of Invention in Composition*

ANIS S. BAWARSHI

UTAH STATE UNIVERSITY PRESS
*Logan, Utah*

Utah State University Press
Logan, Utah 84322-7800

Manufactured in the United States of America.
Cover design by Barbara Yale-Read.

Library of Congress Cataloging-in-Publication Data

Bawarshi, Anis S.
  Genre and the invention of the writer : reconsidering the place of
invention in composition / Anis Bawarshi.
      p. cm.
Includes bibliographical references and index.
  ISBN 0-87421-554-4 (pbk. : alk. paper)
  1. English language—Rhetoric—Study and teaching. 2. English
language—Composition and exercises—Study and teaching. 3. Invention
(Rhetoric) 4. Literary form. I. Title.
  PE1404 .B34 2003
  808'.02—dc21
                              2002153375

*To*
AMY FELDMAN
*and to*
BIKO *and* SWEETPEA

*In memory of*
ASHLEY

*All my love*

# CONTENTS

# PREFACE

The preface harbors a lie.

GAYATRI SPIVAK, Preface to *Of Grammatology*

A preface precedes a book that likely has been written prior to it, thus making it a discursive move doomed to fail from the start. That is in part the lie it harbors. But as Spivak reminds us, this lie a preface harbors is more than an accepted, amusing fiction readers live with; the presence of a preface also upsets a book's desire to stand alone, self-made, an object that is its own explanation. It fractures that desired autonomy by reminding us that a writer and text are never alone; they are deferred, always preceded and surrounded by and always building on and adding to other writers and texts. In her own translator's preface to Derrida's preface to *Of Grammatology*, Spivak writes that "the text has no stable identity, no stable origin, no stable end. Each act of reading the 'text' is a preface to the next" (1976, x). A preface is thus an act of repetition that unhinges and defers the thing it repeats at the same time as it inaugurates and promotes it.

I read this relationship between a book and its preface as somewhat analogous to the project this book attempts to undertake. In examining the dynamic relationship between writers and the texts they produce, I am interested in how writers both preface a text and are prefaced by other texts, namely genres, in relation to which they write. As such, the act of writing becomes a complex site for the enactment of prefaces, in which writers and texts preface each other, constantly inaugurating and deferring their own beginnings. In this book, I identify genres as such sites of interaction in which, to paraphrase Louis Althusser (1984), writers act as they are acted upon. In its examination of this process of articulation, I hope the book can contribute something of importance and of use to the study and teaching of invention and writing in composition studies.

Situated at the intersection between acting and being acted upon, I would like here to take the opportunity the preface allows to identify and thank those who, through their support, expertise, direction, and generosity, have acted upon me to make this book possible.

It was my teacher and mentor and more recently my coauthor and friend at the University of Kansas, Amy J. Devitt, who first introduced me to genre eight years ago and who helped me formulate the questions I continue to ask to this day. This book is the gift of expert knowledge, wise direction, and unwavering support and patience she has given me over the years, and in whatever are its strengths, this book is the gift I give back to her. At the University of Kansas, I also benefited in countless and lasting ways from the wisdom and knowledge of my teachers: Peter Casagrande, who shared and guided my curiosity into why and how texts are produced; James Hartman, through whose careful and thoughtful questions I learned to think more carefully and thoughtfully; and Sidney I. Dobrin, whose expertise, vision, and energy inform my work to this day. For his early mentorship while I was an undergraduate, I thank Gale K. Larson.

In addition to the scholarship that has shaped my thinking before and during the writing of this book, my work has profited in countless ways over the years from interactions with and the support of friends and colleagues. Among those, I would like especially to thank Mary Jo Reiff, who continues to enrich my work through her insight and unfailing collaboration. Thank you also to Andrea Lunsford, who read portions of the manuscript and whose timely and sage advice turned out to be a turning point in my revisions. At the University of Washington, I am particularly grateful to Anne Curzan for reading and offering valuable feedback on the manuscript as well as for her camaraderie and support; to Chandan Reddy for his extraordinary attentiveness and generous contribution when I was working through key questions and ideas; to my colleagues in language and rhetoric: George Dillon, Joan Graham, Juan Guerra, Sandra Silberstein, Gail Stygall, and John Webster for their knowledge and guidance; to Marshall Brown for reading and commenting on portions of the manuscript; to Kimberly Emmons, Steven Johnson, Catherine McDonald, Terri Major, and Spencer Schaffner for sharing materials, ideas, and questions from their writing courses and research; and to Ann Wennerstrom as well as the students in my graduate seminars on genre theory in Winter 2000 and Winter 2002, whose elegant questions and thoughtful inquiry encouraged me to ask new questions and to think more deeply about genre. At the University of Washington, I am grateful for the support of a research quarter in Spring 2002 and summer research support in Summer 2002 as part of the Junior Faculty Development Program, both of which enabled me to complete this book.

Michael Spooner, director of Utah State University Press, has made the revising of this book a gratifying and rewarding experience. Thanks also to Charles Bazerman and the anonymous reviewers at USUP for their constructive and encouraging comments. At USUP, the manuscript has been fortunate to receive the expert copyediting of Tyler Leary and typesetting of Ian Hatch. For granting permission to reprint portions of previously published material in chapters 2 and 4, I thank the publishers of *College English* (NCTE) and the edited book collection *Ecocomposition: Theoretical and Pedagogical Approaches* (SUNY).

Finally, I would like to thank my family and friends for their love, understanding, good humor, and constant support. With love and admiration, I thank Amy Feldman, who read and offered valuable feedback on several drafts of the manuscript, and who, along the way, handled my doubts and questions with extraordinary loving-kindness. Her presence gives me a place to be outside of this book, and I am grateful to her for that. And, to the beginnings, to my mother and father, whose sacrifice and courage have taught me most of all how to be thankful. I act in ways they have acted on me.

# 1

## INTRODUCTION
### A Meditation on Beginnings

A beginning is that which does not itself follow
anything by causal necessity, but after which something
naturally is or comes to be.

ARISTOTLE, *Poetics*

My way is to begin with the beginning.

LORD BYRON, *Don Juan*

The speaker is not the biblical Adam, dealing only with
virgin and still unnamed objects, giving them names
for the first time.

M. M. BAKHTIN, *Speech Genres*

Writers are . . . different from the subjects of the
composing processes we often describe, for they do not
generate, transcribe, and fix meanings independently
from the systems of language and cultural history that
equally participate in these processes.

SUSAN MILLER, *Rescuing the Subject*

Perhaps the most appropriate way to begin this book is by asking
what it means to begin, because in many ways this book is about
beginnings, about *why* and *how* writers begin to write, and about
the ways we in composition studies imagine, study, and teach how,
why, and where writing begins—the subject of invention. It
attempts to locate and describe where invention takes place and
what happens *to* writers when they begin to write. In so doing, this
book extends the question, "what do writers *do* when they write?"
by asking, "what happens *to* writers that motivates them to do what
they do?" Framed in this way, the question invites us to examine
invention not only as a site for the writer's articulation of desire,

but also as a site for the writer's acquisition of desire. Recent scholarship in genre theory can contribute a great deal to such an understanding of invention, and in the chapters that follow, I will describe that contribution and explore what is at stake for the study and teaching of writing to imagine invention in this way.

But how can we begin to write about beginnings? Where do we begin? We could, as Byron suggests, begin with the beginning, the scene of origin that, according to Aristotle, "does not itself follow anything by causal necessity." Rejecting the *in medias res* (the "into the midst of things") strategy with which traditional epic poems begin, Byron announces that he will begin his epic poem, *Don Juan*, at the beginning, with the birth of his hero. Don Juan was born in Seville, Byron tells us; his father "traced his source/Through the most Gothic gentlemen of Spain," while his mother's "memory was a mine." Yet the fact that Don Juan is born in Seville, the fact of his father's lineage and his mother's memory—all these preclude any sense of a beginning unpreceded by "causal necessity." As soon as Byron announces his intention to begin with the beginning, he (perhaps unwittingly but more likely satirically) reveals the impossibility of beginning as such. The beginning of *Don Juan* is, in a very real sense, already in medias res, already taking place in the midst of things.

Such is the ironic nature of beginnings, performing at once an act of initiation and an act of continuation. This introduction— this beginning of the book—is a case in point. It initiates the book that follows, but it is also what Edward Said calls an "effort on behalf of discursive continuity" (1975, 69). That is, it sets up what is to follow at the same time as it situates what follows in the midst of what already exists, the "systems of language and cultural history" represented in part by the texts of Aristotle, Byron, Bakhtin, Miller, and the countless other texts that precede, flank, and make possible my own text. Beginnings are acts of departure, but always departures from something, in relation to something, so that, as Bakhtin reminds us, every beginning is a response to a prior beginning (1986). Along with Bakhtin, Said describes beginnings as gestures of continuation, nuanced repetitions, which emerge not linearly but in adjacency to other texts, such that a "text stands to the side of, next to or between the bulk of all other works—not in a line with them, not in a line of descent from them" (1975, 10). Beginnings take place in the midst of things.

To describe beginnings as situated and textured is to describe them in what Said calls secular terms, terms that oppose a view of beginnings as divine or magical acts of unpreceded origination. Such a secular view of beginnings upsets a powerful desire for ultimate origins, what David Bartholomae calls the "desire for an open space, free from the past . . . deployed throughout the discourses of modern life, including the discourses of education" (1995, 64). This desire is particularly strong in the discourses of writing instruction, in which the blank page or computer screen stands symbolic of the open space, the frontier space, from which writers begin. The blank page is mythologized as an unmarked space waiting to be marked, its physical blankness masking the fact of its specification in discursive and ideological conventions, including genres, which already situate it, already mark it.

By and large, the way we imagine invention in writing reflects and enacts this desire for unpreceded beginnings. This desire finds expression in the dozens of self-help writing guides currently lining bookstore shelves that assume the writer as the point of origin for writing, and that purport to teach the aspiring writer how to unleash his or her ideas, voice, and untapped creativity. This desire also finds expression in the countless composition textbooks scattered around writing program offices, some of which are not unlike Marjorie Ford and Jon Ford's *Dreams and Inward Journeys: A Rhetoric and Reader for Writers* (a textbook in its third edition by 1998). In it, the authors tell students that writing is an inward journey, a "process of discovering what resides within your mind and your spirit" (8). They go on to write:

> Many people find it difficult to begin, wondering, perhaps, how they will be able to untangle all of their thoughts and feelings, how they will finally decide on the most accurate words and sentence patterns to make their statements clear and compelling. You may

feel overwhelmed by the possibilities of all that is waiting to be discovered within you, and at the same time you may feel a sense of
wonder and excitement, anticipating pleasures and rewards of
uncovering and expressing new parts of your mind, imagination,
and spirit. (8)

This is, without question, an extreme version of the articulation of this desire, and to say this view reflects current representations of invention in composition textbooks would be unfair and
not altogether accurate.[1] Still, despite the enormous contribution
work on collaboration, intertextuality, and situated cognition has
made to our understanding of the thoroughly social nature of
writing, it is not uncommon for composition textbooks, even
those not designated as "expressivist," routinely to posit invention
as "prewriting," as a practice within the writer that occurs before
and outside the textured midst of things. Indeed, as Rebecca
Moore Howard has recently noted, "one might even go so far as to
say that expressionism is the prevailing model of writing in our
culture" (1999, 47). Invention heuristics such as freewriting,
brainstorming, clustering, and mapping locate the writer as the
primary site and agent of invention.

Various factors account for this "normative model of the
inspired, autonomous author [that] pervades contemporary
pedagogy" (Howard 1999, 57), some of which I will examine in
more detail in chapter 3. Briefly, the pervasive sense that invention, like beginnings, is a scene of origination helps contribute to
the perception that invention is pre-social. This perception holds
that only after something has originated does it become socialized. The scene of origination—the beginnings of a text—that we
popularly designate as invention ostensibly resides before and
somehow remains immune from the social, collaborative, and
discursive conditions that later affect the text's production, circulation, and reception.[2] Likewise, an investment in what Nikolas
Rose has called the "regime of the self" also contributes to this
perception. In *Inventing Ourselves: Psychology, Power, and
Personhood*, Rose examines how psychology as well as other "psy"

fields have invented the intellectual technologies for describing, regulating, and perpetuating the modern Western concept of the person as a locus of self. Such a self is "coherent, bounded, individualized, intentional, the locus of thought, action, and belief, the origin of its own actions, the beneficiary of a unique biography" (1996, 3). In such a fashioning of the self, the writer becomes the identifiable and self-possessed locus of invention, the origin of his or her own desires to act, even, as I will describe in chapter 5, when that desire is obviously prompted by a teacher's writing assignment. Not only is this account of agency politically frustrating; it is also pedagogically limiting when it comes to explaining how and why writers invent.

The "social turn" that has marked much of the scholarship and pedagogy in composition studies over the last twenty years has thoroughly challenged this view of the writer and writing. This social turn recognizes that there is more at work on the text than the writer's seemingly autonomous cognition; there are also various social forces that constitute the scene of production within which the writer's cognition as well as his or her text are situated and shaped. Within composition studies, this scene of writing is commonly (and, some would add, problematically) identified as a discourse community—the social and rhetorical environment within which cognitive habits, goals, assumptions, and values are shared by participants who employ common discourse strategies for communicating and practicing these cognitive habits, goals, assumptions, and values. Guided by an understanding of writing as a social activity, composition scholarship has become less concerned with inquiring into generalizable cognitive processes and more concerned with inquiring into the localized, textured conditions in which cognition and social activities are organized.

As Charles Bazerman explains, such inquiry recognizes writing practices not only as forms of social participation, but also as "integral to . . . complex forms of social organization" (2000, 6). Writing practices situate writers in these forms of participation and organization, so that writers are never alone, even when they are physically alone, and even during invention. In fact, as Richard Young, Alton Becker, and Kenneth Pike demonstrated in their influential book *Rhetoric: Discovery and Change* (1970), invention involves a process of orientation rather than origination. Young, Becker, and Pike's tagmemic rhetoric and their elegant and complex heuristic of particle, wave, and field presents a set of questions that enable writers to examine a rhetorical situation from various perspectives. Their heuristic framework orients writers in the midst of a rhetorical situation, and the eventual problems writers formulate and analyze as well as the eventual choices that writers make in relation to these problems emerge out of this orientation. Young, Becker, and Pike's tagmemic rhetoric, along with Richard Young's (1978; 1986; 1994) and Janice Lauer's (1967; 1970; 1984) influential work on invention, teaches us that invention is less an inspired, mysterious activity and more a location and mode of inquiry, a way of positioning oneself in relation to a problem and a way of working through it.

Karen Burke LeFevre's *Invention as a Social Act* (1987), building on and adding to the work of Young and Lauer, turns to research in linguistics, creativity theory, sociology, philosophy, and psychology to examine the thoroughly social and interpersonal nature of invention. Toward the end of the book, LeFevre calls for continued social-based research into invention, research that examines "a larger locus of inventive activity, a social matrix rather than an isolated writer and text" (1987, 125). She writes: "we should study the ecology of invention—the ways ideas arise and are nurtured or hindered by interaction with social context and culture" (126). A number of scholars, to varying degrees and with different agendas, have since taken up this study of invention and authorship, including Brodkey (1987), Bleich (1988), S. Miller (1989), Cooper and Holzman (1989), Crowley (1990), Ede and Lunsford (1990), Faigley (1992), Flower (1994), Berlin (1996), Howard (1999), and Halasek (1999). In this book, I build on and add to these studies by responding in particular to LeFevre's call for inquiry into the ecology of invention, which calls for "re-*placing*" invention in a social and rhetorical scene that shapes and is shaped by it. Turning to recent scholarship in genre theory, I examine invention as the site in which writers act within and are acted upon by the social and rhetorical conditions that we call genres—the site in which writers acquire, negotiate, and articulate the desires to write. Genres, which Carolyn Miller (1984) has defined as typified rhetorical ways of acting in recurring situations, position and condition discursive behavior in such a way as to preclude a sense of beginnings as unpreceded, unmediated, unmarked scenes of origin. If beginnings take place in the textured midst of things, as the aforementioned scholarship on invention argues, then genres are part of this midst of things, rhetorically sustaining and enabling the ways communicants recognize and act in various situations. Writers invent within genres and are themselves invented by genres. In arguing that genres are places in which invention (and writers) take place, I hope to contribute to and enrich our understanding of invention in composition studies.

When I began my research for this book a few years ago, my father asked me what I was studying. I told him, "Genre." Looking puzzled, he said, "Jon-ra?" I said, "Yes, jon-ra." Then, in an attempted French accent, he said, "Oh you mean genrrrr," rolling the r at the end. My brother, who was listening nearby, asked, "What is genre?" In all seriousness and without hesitating, my father replied, "Nothing; genre is nothing. You are writing a book about nothing?" Academics' sensitivity to the charge that we study "nothing" notwithstanding, my father's claim about genre was not unfounded. After all, the word *genre*, borrowed from French, means "sort" or "kind," and to study sorts or kinds of things (inherently an abstract notion) is not as substantial as, say, studying the things themselves. Certainly, genre appears to be nothing when it is defined as a way of innocently classifying or sorting kinds of texts. But in the past two decades, scholarship in genre theory has come a long way in dispelling the notion that genres are merely artificial and arbitrary systems of classification, positing instead that genres are dynamic discursive formations in which ideology is naturalized and realized in specific social actions, relations, and subjectivities. Indeed, genre is not nothing.

Genre is not nothing in the same way that beginnings are not preceded by nothing, a way of moving from nothing to something. A genre is not simply a classification, a way of describing something that is produced before or outside of its rhetorical and conceptual framework. As I will describe in chapter 2, genres *function* on their writers, readers, and contexts. Indeed, one of the roots of the word *genre*, by way of its related word *gender*, can be traced to the Latin cognate *gener*, meaning to generate. This etymology suggests that genre both *sorts* and *generates*. As such, what makes genre significant to a study of invention is not so much that it functions as a site in which the thing invented gets placed in order to be identified, but that genre functions as a site in which invention *itself* takes place. In this formulation, genre becomes akin to what Pierre Bourdieu calls "habitus," which he defines as "structured structures predisposed to function as structuring structures, that is, as principles which *generate* and *organize* practices and representations" (1990, 53). Like habitus, genre both organizes and generates the conditions of social and rhetorical production. The function of a genre only seems like nothing when we, through practice and socialization, have internalized its ideology in the form of rhetorical conventions to such an extent that our invention of a text seems to emanate independently and introspectively, even almost intuitively, from us. Indeed, as we will examine later, the power of genre resides, in part, in this ideological sleight of hand, in which social obligation to act becomes internalized as self-generated desire to act in certain rhetorical ways.

Insofar as genres are structuring as well as structured structures, they can be metaphorically described as rhetorical ecosystems. There are several reasons why I find this metaphor useful and why I take it up in later chapters. For one thing, it suggests that generic boundaries are not simply classificatory constraints within which writers and speakers function; rather, these boundaries are social and rhetorical conditions which make possible certain commitments, relations, and actions. Just as natural ecosystems sustain certain forms of life, so genres maintain rhetorical conditions that sustain certain forms of life—ways of discursively and materially organizing, knowing, experiencing, acting, and relating in the world. More significantly, the metaphor also captures the dynamic relationship between rhetorical habits and social habitats that genres maintain. It suggests that, rather than being static backdrops against which speakers and writers act, social and rhetorical conditions are constantly being reproduced and transformed as speakers and writers act within them. By way of genres, speakers and writers maintain the habitual social and rhetorical interactions and practices that sustain the social and rhetorical conditions that in turn compel such habitual interactions and practices. Just as ecosystems maintain a symbiotic relationship between organisms and their habitats, with habitats being sustained by the very organisms that they sustain, so too genres are sustained by the very writers that they sustain. As such, genres organize the conditions of production as well as generate the rhetorical articulation of these conditions, reciprocally. Which is another way of saying that genres maintain the desires that they help writers fulfill.

Genres are places of articulation. They are ideological configurations that are realized in their articulation, as they are used by writers (and readers). Genres also place writers in positions of articulation. Here we discern the dynamic, seemingly paradoxical, relationship between writers and genres, one that we will examine more closely in chapter 4. Genres exist because writers produce them, but writers produce them because genres already exist. In this formulation, the notion of agency becomes more complicated, requiring us to examine more closely how and why we are motivated to act. Kenneth Burke, in *A Grammar of Motives*, describes how this paradoxical relationship is at the heart of his attempt to explain the drama of motive:

> We may discern a dramatistic pun, involving a merger of active and passive in the expression, "the motivation to act." Strictly speaking,

the act of an agent would be the movement not of one *moved* but of a *mover* (a mover of the self or of something else by the self). For an act is by definition active, whereas to be moved (or motivated) is by definition passive. Thus, if we quizzically scrutinize the expression, "the motivation to act," we note that it implicitly contains the paradox of substance . . . to consider an *act* in terms of its grounds is to consider it in terms of what it is not, namely, in terms of motives that, in acting upon the active, would make it a kind of passive. We could state the paradox another way by saying that the concept of activation implies a kind of passive-behind-the-passive; for an agent who is "motivated by his passions" would be "moved by his being-moved-ness," or "acted upon by his state of being acted upon." (1969a, 40)

For Burke, then, the motivation to act captures the paradox of articulation, namely that writers articulate genres as they are articulated by genres. This scene of articulation takes place within genres, and has a great deal to offer to the way we study and teach invention in composition studies.

There is, of course, a chicken-and-egg dilemma at work in all this, but attempting to address it is beyond the scope of this book. Ultimately, I am less interested in the "time before genre"—that time no longer exists—and more interested in what happens once genres are in circulation, because it is there that the dynamic relation between writers and genres always already exists and affects future actions. In particular, I am interested in how and why already existing genres not only enable individuals to shape social and rhetorical practices, but also to transform them, so that new genres emerge out of contact with those already in use, and evolve as they reflect changing values and assumptions (see for instance Popken's 1999 research into the evolution of the resume and Bazerman's 1988 research into the evolution of the experimental article). As such, I am interested in the synchronic relationship between genres and writers, especially the ways this relationship gets enacted during the scene of invention, where genre knowledge becomes a form of what Berkenkotter and Huckin call "situated cognition" (1993, 485).

To think of genre knowledge as situated, textured cognition is to implicate genre in the formation and negotiation of subjectivity and desire (Fuller and Lee 2002, 211), which is what makes genre such a useful site for investigating invention. In arguing that invention begins and takes place within the social and rhetorical conditions constituted by genres, however, I do not presume that genres are the only sites in which writers invent, nor do I suggest that genres are entirely deterministic. Genres themselves take place within what Bakhtin calls larger "spheres of culture" (1986), what Freadman calls "ceremonials" (1988), and what Russell, borrowing from activity theory, calls "activity systems" (1997). Within these larger spheres of language and activity, writers negotiate multiple, sometimes conflicting genres, relations, and subjectivities, so that there is always the potential, in some genres and in some situations more than others, for generic resistance and hybridization. Indeed, as I will discuss in chapter 4, the articulation of genre is also the possibility of its transformation. In addition, various other forces are also at work shaping how and why writers invent, including economic conditions; power relations; racial, ethnic, class, and gender formations; material and geographic conditions; libidinal attachments; not to mention biological and other x-factors. I cannot and do not claim, then, that genres account entirely for how and why writers invent. What I do claim is that genres reveal and help us map part of what LeFevre calls the "ecology of invention," hence allowing us to locate a writer's motives to act within typified rhetorical and social conditions. In giving us access to the ecology of invention, genres can provide a richer account of agency as well as a more useful means for describing and teaching invention.

In later chapters, I will consider in more detail how different genres constitute writers into different subject formations, and what these formations reveal about how and why writers invent. Along the way, I will examine the position of the writer as someone who not only writes, but who is also "written" or produced by the genres that he or she writes. I am curious about what happens to writers as they write—what positions they are asked to assume, how and why they represent their activities, themselves, and others rhetorically, how they act as they are acted upon, what tensions exist between a writer's intentions and a genre's social motives, and how these tensions get played out as social and rhetorical practices. Such questions appear increasingly relevant to the work of composition theory and pedagogy. These questions challenge scholars and teachers of writing to examine not only the complex processes involved in the *production of the text* and its consequences (what writers do when they write and its effects), but also the complex processes involved in the *production of the writer* and its consequences (what is done to writers when they write and its effects). We cannot, I argue, fully understand or answer the question "what do writers *do* when they write?" without understanding and answering the question "what happens *to* writers when they write?" In genre theory, I see a way to bring these questions together, to account not only for how writers articulate motives or desires, but also for how writers obtain motives or desires to write—how, that is, writers both invent and are invented by the genres that they write.

Chapter 2 introduces the concept of genre, tracing its development through literary studies up to its more recent reconceptualizations in applied linguistics, communication studies, rhetoric, and composition. Bringing together definitions of genre from various disciplines, this chapter presents what I will be calling the "genre function," a term borrowed from Foucault's concept of the author-function to describe genres as constitutive (that is, both regulative and generative) of social and rhetorical actions, relations, and identities. Such a view of genre will serve as a framework for examining invention and the writer in later chapters.

In chapter 3, I will consider the various views of the writer that have dominated the study and teaching of writing since the late eighteenth century, especially how these views of the writer continue to be reflected in what Sharon Crowley and Karen Burke LeFevre have described as composition studies' introspective theories of invention. In particular, I will investigate the role that the "process movement" has played in shaping our views of the writer as "author" over the last forty years, views that have contributed to a privatization of invention from a social and rhetorical act to an individual and introspective act. By and large, writing instruction continues to treat the writer as its point of departure, and this chapter will consider what such a treatment has meant for the ways we define writing and its instruction, and what it would mean to rethink the writer and invention as a result.

Analyzing the relationship between genre and subject formation, I locate invention at the intersection between the acquisition and articulation of desire—the site at which writers obtain, negotiate, and enact specific social commitments, orientations, and relations within what Bazerman has recently called "genred" discursive spaces (2002, 15). Chapter 4 locates the figure of the writer within these genred discursive spaces, demonstrating in theory and with examples how and why writers are produced by the genres they write. Drawing on the work of the sociologist Anthony Giddens, chapter 4 describes the role that genres play in reproducing the situational motives that writers internalize as intentions and actualize as socio-rhetorical actions and identities in such varied examples as the Patient Medical History Form, the state of the union address, social work assessment reports, and greeting cards.

In chapter 5, I will consider genres as situated topoi within which invention takes place, habits as well as habitats for acting in language. I will describe and analyze the first-year writing (FYW) classroom as an activity system shaped and enabled by various genres, each of which constitutes its own topoi within which teachers and students assume and enact a complex set of social actions, relations, and positions. In particular, I will analyze the syllabus, the writing prompt, and, its uptake, the student essay, in order to counter misconceptions that the FYW classroom is an artificial environment within which writing takes place. Actually, like any other environment, the FYW classroom is a multilayered, multitextured site of social and material action and identity formation, a site that is reproduced as it is rhetorically enacted by its participants within the various classroom genres available to them. By studying the relationship between the writing prompt and the student essay, for example, we can observe the complex relations and repositioning that students must negotiate as they transition from one genred discursive space to another. Invention takes place at the nexus where prompt and essay meet, and in chapter 5, I examine how students negotiate this discursive transaction by recontextualizing the desires embedded in the writing prompt as their own self-sponsored desires in their essays. Analyzing the syllabus, writing prompt, and student essay as sites of invention gives us insight into how students and teachers (re)position themselves as social actors within at the same time as they enact the activity system we call FYW.

Writing takes place. It takes place socially and rhetorically. To write is to position oneself within genres—to assume and enact certain situated commitments, identities, relations, and practices. In the final chapter, I will consider the implications of making this positioning visible and accessible to students, implications which invite us to rethink not only our teaching practices in writing courses, including the ways we teach invention, but also our goals for writing instruction. I offer genre analysis as a way for students to access, position themselves within, and participate critically in genred discursive spaces and the commitments, relations, identities, and activities embedded within them. Along the way, I will argue that this approach challenges us to teach writing not so much as "composition" but as rhetoric—as a way of being and acting in the world, socially and rhetorically, within genres—and then I will speculate on what it would mean, especially for writing in the disciplines (WID) initiatives, to teach FYW in this way.

Today, perhaps more than ever, the place of composition is contested. Among those who study and teach composition in the university, some justify the place of composition within English departments while others argue that composition needs to forge its own interdisciplinary identity—its own place—either as its own department outside of English or as part of WID programs. These are pressing and significant debates about the institutional place of composition, and they will continue to shape the teaching and professional identity of composition studies in the U.S. Yet these debates about the institutional *place of composition*, debates which have motivated a great deal of scholarly work in composition studies and contributed in large part to the field's self-definition, can also be fruitfully read in relation to where *composition takes place*, particularly the beginnings of composition, the locus of invention. At the end of the book, I will address the place of composition within the university (the institutional place of writing); in the rest of the book, I will define "the place of composition" to mean the genred scenes in which writers invent and write. By examining these scenes for what they can tell us about how agency operates, we stand to gain a richer and I hope a more pedagogically useful understanding of invention, the writer, and their place of composition.

# 2

## THE GENRE FUNCTION

[W]hat we learn when we learn a genre is not just a
pattern of forms or even a method of achieving our
own ends. We learn, more importantly, what ends we
may have. . . . As a recurrent, significant action, a
genre embodies an aspect of cultural rationality.

CAROLYN MILLER, "Genre as Social Action"

We are written only as we write, by the agency within us
which always already keeps watch over perception, be it
internal or external. The "subject" of writing does not
exist if we mean by that some sovereign solitude of the
author. The subject of writing is a system of relations
between strata: the Mystic Pad, the psyche, society, the
world. Within that scene, on that stage, the punctual
simplicity of the classical subject is not to be found.

JACQUES DERRIDA, "Freud and the Scene of Writing"

At the beginning of *A Grammar of Motives*, Kenneth Burke wonders: "What is involved, when we say what people are doing and
why they are doing it?" (1969a, xv). Burke describes and locates
this question of motive in a dramatistic pentad made up of scene
(where an action takes place), act (what is taking place), agent
(who is performing the action), agency (how, through what
means, is the action carried out), and purpose (why is the action
being carried out). Motive, he explains, does not reside in the
agent alone, a romantic concept, but in the relationships
between all five terms of the pentad, all of which conspire to
define and enact the drama of motive. Within the scope of this
book, I essentially ask the same question as it applies to the study
and teaching of invention in composition studies: what is
involved when we say what writers are doing and why they are
doing it? In response, I answer that *genre* is involved. Genres are

discursive sites that coordinate the acquisition and production of motives by maintaining specific relations between scene, act, agent, agency, and purpose. And when writers begin to write in different genres, they participate within these different sets of relations, relations that motivate them, consciously or unconsciously, to invent both their texts and themselves. In this way, genre functions as what Miller calls "an aspect of cultural rationality" (C. Miller 1984, 165), a "stabilized-for-now or stabilized-enough site of social and ideological action" (Schryer 1994, 107) in which writers acquire and articulate motives to write. In this chapter I turn to scholarship in literary theory, applied linguistics, and rhetoric and composition to describe genres as such sites of action.[1] Then in later chapters I will examine how writers get positioned within and negotiate these sites of action, and will consider the ways this positioning can inform our understanding of invention as well as our study and teaching of writing.

The past twenty years have witnessed a dramatic reconceptualization of genre and its role in the production and interpretation of texts and culture. Led in large part by scholars in applied linguistics (Bhatia, Freedman, Halliday, Kress, Martin, Medway, Swales), communication studies (Yates and Orlikowski), education (Christie, Dias, Paré), and rhetoric and composition studies (Bazerman, Berkenkotter, Campbell, Coe, Devitt, Giltrow, Jamieson, C. Miller, Russell, Schryer), this movement has helped transform genre study from a descriptive to an explanatory activity, one that investigates not only text-types and classification systems, but also the linguistic, sociological, and psychological assumptions underlying and shaping these text-types. No longer mainly used to structure and classify a literary textual universe as Northrop Frye (1957) and others in literary studies have traditionally offered, genres have come to be defined as typified rhetorical strategies communicants use to recognize, organize, and act in all kinds of situations, literary and nonliterary. As such, there is a growing sense among those who study genre that genres do not just help us define and organize kinds of texts; they also help us define and organize kinds of situations and social actions, situations and actions that the genres, through their use, rhetorically make possible. This notion of genre as a dynamic site for the production and regulation of textured, ideological activities (a site in which habitual language practices enact and reproduce situated relations, commitments, and actions) has a great deal to offer to the study and teaching of invention in composition studies. For instance, by maintaining the desires they help to fulfill, genres provide a way for us to interrogate analytically how writers get positioned within these textured desires to act at the same time as they enable writers to articulate and fulfill these desires as recognizable, meaningful, consequential actions. It is the overall argument of this book that we can and should make these "genred" discursive spaces (Bazerman 2002, 17) visible to students, not only for the sake of fostering in students a critical awareness of what genres help us do and not do, but also for the sake of enabling students to participate in these spaces more meaningfully and critically.

To make such a claim for genre, to argue that genres are sites for literate, ideological action, is to endow genre with a status that will surely make some readers uneasy. After all, in literary studies, genre has traditionally occupied a subservient role to the writer and the text he or she produces, at best used as a classificatory device or an a posteriori interpretive tool in relation to already existing texts and motives, and at worst censured as formulaic writing. Suffice it to say, genre has not enjoyed very good standing in literary studies, particularly since the late eighteenth century when interest in literary "kinds" gave way to a concern for literary "texts" and their writers, a shift that can be characterized as moving from "poetics" to the poem and the poet. So it is not surprising that the work done to reconceptualize genre over the last twenty years has come predominantly from scholars working outside of literary studies, scholars who are interested in how and why typified texts reflect and organize everyday social occasions and practices.[2] It is their work, with its basis in applied linguistics and sociology, that informs a great deal of the theoretical underpinnings for this book. This chapter will examine some of these underpinnings. But breaking with what has become common practice in nonliterary reconceptualizations of genre—or what is becoming referred to as "rhetorical genre studies"—I do not want to ignore literary considerations of genre or, for that matter, to argue that literary theories of genre are inimical to rhetorical theories of genre. Instead, by reviewing more recent studies of genre by literary scholars alongside studies of genre by scholars in rhetoric, composition, and applied linguistics, I hope to demonstrate how much literary and rhetorical theories of genre have to contribute to one another, indeed, how when we build on the knowledge of both, we can measure the extent to which genres are constitutive both of literary and nonliterary contexts as well as of literary and nonliterary writers. Putting literary and rhetorical theories of genre in dialogue with one another will allow us to see how all genres, far from being transparent lenses for identifying and organizing texts, indeed function as sites in which communicants use language to make certain situated activities possible. Since genres locate all writers within such situated language practices, ideologies, and activities, they enable us to examine more fully the "social organization of cognition" (Bazerman 1997a, 305)—the conditions and assumptions that shape the choices writers make when they begin to write, conditions and assumptions that, as I will explore in later chapters, will shed more light on the study and teaching of invention.

## FROM AUTHOR FUNCTION TO GENRE FUNCTION

In describing genres as sites of action, I build on what Michel Foucault calls the "author-function" in order to describe how the same principles that govern literary activity, when expanded from the author to the genre function, are at work governing a wider range of socio-discursive activity. In "What Is an Author?" Foucault attempts to locate and articulate the "space left empty by the author's disappearance" (1994, 345) in structuralist and poststructuralist literary theory. If the author can no longer be said to constitute a work, Foucault wonders, then what does? What is it that delimits discourse so that it becomes recognized as a work which has certain value and status? Sans the author, in short, what is it that plays "the role of the regulator of the fictive" (353)? For Foucault, the answer is the "author-function." The author-function does not refer to the "real" writer, the individual with the proper name who precedes and exists independently of the work. Instead, it refers to the author's name, which, in addition to being a proper name, is also a literary name, a name that exists only in relation to the work associated with it. The author-function, then, endows a work with a certain cultural status and value. At the same time, the author-function also endows the idea of "author" with a certain cultural status and value. So the author-function not only constitutes the work as having a certain cultural capital; it also constitutes the producer of that work into the privileged role of "author" as opposed to the real writer with "just a proper name like the rest" (345).

The author-function delimits what works we recognize as valuable and how we interpret them at the same time as it accords the status of author to certain writers: "these aspects of an individual which we designate as making him an author are only a projection, in more or less psychologizing terms, of the operations that we force texts to undergo . . ." (Foucault 347). The role of author, therefore, becomes akin to a subject position regulated, as much as the work itself, by the author-function. Constituted by the author-function, the "real writer" becomes positioned as an "author," "a variable and complex function of discourse" (352). In this position, "the author does not precede the works[;] he is a certain functional principle by which, in our culture, one limits, excludes, and chooses; in short, by which one impedes the free circulation, the free manipulation, the free composition, decomposition, and recomposition of fiction" (352–53).

Symbolically as well as materially, the author-function helps delimit what Foucault calls a "certain discursive construct" (346) within which a work and its author function, so that the way we recognize a certain text and its author as deserving of a privileged status—a text worthy of our study, say, rather than "simply" to be "used"—is regulated by the author-function. Not only does the author-function, then, play a classificatory role, helping us organize and define texts (346); more significantly, Foucault argues, it marks off "the edges of the text, revealing, or at least characterizing, its *mode of being*. The author's name manifests the appearance of a certain discursive set and indicates the status of this discourse within a society and a culture" (346; my emphasis). Insofar as the author-function characterizes a text's "mode of being," it constitutes it and its author, providing a text and its author with a cultural identity and significance not accorded to texts that exist outside of its purview. As Foucault explains, "The author-function is . . . characteristic of the mode of existence, circulation, and functioning of *certain* discourses within a society" (346; my emphasis). For example, he identifies such texts as private letters and contracts, even though they are written by some*one*, as not having "authors," and, as such, as not constituted by the author-function, ostensibly meaning that their mode of being is regulated not by an author's name but by some other function.

In English studies, we use the author-function to designate certain works we call "literary," works most often recognized, valued, and interpreted in relation to their authors' names, which become cultural values we ascribe to these works. So, for example, a traditional literary scholar might state, "I study D. H. Lawrence" or "I am reading a lot of Virginia Woolf these days," whereas a scholar in rhetoric and composition, say, might more likely state, "I am studying the research article." Not only does the author-function privilege the author to the exclusion of genre, but in using it to characterize and clarify only certain discourses' modes of existence, we also stand to ignore a great many other discourses and their existence, in particular, how and why nonliterary discourses assume certain cultural values and regulate their users' social positions, relations, and identities in certain ways. Foucault describes, for instance, how the author-function, endowing a certain text with an author-value, "shows that this discourse is not ordinary everyday speech that merely comes and goes, not something that is immediately consumable. On the contrary, it is a speech that must be received in a certain mode and that, in a given culture, must receive a certain status" (346). But what about the "everyday speech *that merely comes and goes?*" Since it does not exist within the realm of the author-function, what is it that regulates such discourse? We need a concept that can account not only for how certain privileged discourses function, but for how all discourses function, an overarching concept that can explain the social roles we assign to various discourses and those who enact and are enacted by them. Genre *is* such a concept. Within each genre, discourse is "received in a certain mode" and "must receive a certain status," including even discourse endowed with an author-function. In fact, it is quite possible that the author-function is itself a function of literary genres, which create the ideological conditions that produce this subject we call an "author." And so, I propose to subsume what Foucault calls the author-function within what I am calling the *genre function*, which constitutes all discourses' and all writers' modes of existence, circulation, and functioning within a society, whether the writer is William Shakespeare or a social worker and whether the text is a sonnet or an assessment report.

Just as the author-function delimits how individuals conceptually value and materially use certain discourses, I argue that the genre function also delimits discursive action both conceptually and materially. As a site of action, genre is both a concept and its material articulation and exchange. On one level, genre functions as part of what Berkenkotter and Huckin call individuals' "situated cognition" (1993, 485). A genre conceptually frames what its users generally imagine as possible within a given situation, predisposing them to act in certain ways by rhetorically framing how they come to know and respond to certain situations. Genres help endow situations with a "logic" or "common sense." But genres do not only function conceptually. It is in their material manifestations—their modus operandi—that genres exist.

Genres function in the social practices that they help generate and organize, in the unfolding of material, everyday exchanges of language practices, activities, and relations by and between individuals in specific settings. It is in such actual uses of language, uses endowed with material consequences and meaning within different genres, that genres appear and operate. The genre function, then, comes to be and structures social action through its use, through the way its users play its language game. In such a sense is genre both and at once a concept and a material practice, framing our dispositions to act as well as enabling us to articulate and exchange these dispositions as language practices.[3]

The genre function, thus, constitutes how individuals come to conceptualize and act within different situations, framing not only what Foucault calls a discourse's mode of being, but also the mode of being of those who participate in the discourse. Such inquiry into the social mode of being of discourse and its participants has driven much of the work in genre studies, especially since Carolyn Miller's ground-breaking article, "Genre as Social Action," first appeared in 1984. Based in part on Miller's work and the work of Karlyn Kohrs Campbell and Kathleen M. Jamieson (1978), Kenneth Burke (1969b), Lloyd F. Bitzer (1968), and M. A. K. Halliday (1978) whose work Miller extends, genre theorists have begun to question traditional views of genres as simply innocent, artificial, and even arbitrary forms that contain ideas. This container view of genre, which assumes that genres are only transparent and innocent conduits that individuals use to package their communicative goals, overlooks the socio-rhetorical function of genres—the extent to which genres shape and help us generate our communicative goals, including why these goals exist, what and whose purposes they serve, and how best to achieve them. Carolyn Miller, for example, defines genres as "typified rhetorical *actions* based in recurrent situations" (1984, 159; my emphasis). In so doing, Miller shifts the focus of genre study from shared features to shared actions, so that genres come to be defined not just by their typified features but also by the typified actions they make happen. She argues that genres are not only typified rhetorical responses to recurrent situations; they also help shape and maintain the ways we rhetorically know and act within these situations. In other words, as individuals' rhetorical responses to recurrent situations become typified as genres, the genres in turn help structure the way individuals conceptualize and experience these situations, predicting their notions of what constitutes appropriate and possible responses and actions. This is why genres are both functional and epistemological—they help us function within particular situations at the same time as they help shape the ways we come to know and organize these situations.

To argue that genres help reproduce the very recurring situations to which they respond (Devitt 1993) is to identify them as constitutive rather than as merely regulative, which is also what Foucault was claiming for the author-function. John Searle distinguishes between regulative and constitutive rules as follows: "Regulative rules regulate a pre-existing activity, an activity whose existence is logically independent of the rules. Constitutive rules constitute (and also regulate) an activity, the existence of which is logically dependent on the rules" (1969, 34). Those scholars who define genre as regulative perceive it, at best, as being a communicative or interpretive tool, a lens for framing and identifying an already existing communicative activity (see, for example, Hirsch 1967 and Rosmarin 1985 in literary studies; Bhatia 1993 and Swales 1990 in linguistics), and, at worst, an artificial, restrictive "law" that interferes with or tries to trap communicative activity (Blanchot 1959, Croce 1968, Derrida 1980, to name just a few). As Devitt and Miller argue, however, and as I will demonstrate in later examples, genre does not simply *regulate* a pre-existing social activity; instead, it *constitutes* the activity by making it possible by way of its ideological and discursive conventions. In fact, genre reproduces the activity by providing individuals with the conventions for enacting it. We perform an activity in terms of how we recognize it—that is, how we identify and come to know it. And one of the ways we recognize an activity is by way of the genres that constitute it. Genres help organize and generate our social actions by rhetorically constituting the way we recognize the situations within which we function. In short, genres maintain the desires they help fulfill.

Charles Bazerman, in his recent "The Life of Genre, the Life in the Classroom," articulates a similar view of genres as sites of action. He writes:

> Genres are not just forms. Genres are forms of life, ways of being. They are frames for social action. They are environments for learning. They are locations within which meaning is constructed. Genres shape the thoughts we form and the communications by which we interact. Genres are the familiar places we go to create intelligible communicative action with each other and the guideposts we use to explore the unfamiliar. (1997b, 19)

Indeed, genres play a role in helping us organize, experience, and potentially change the situations within which we communicate by functioning at the intersection between the acquisition and articulation of desires to act. Genres shape us as we give shape to them, which is why they constitute our activities and regulate how and why we perform them. In this way, we can attribute to the genre function many of the claims Foucault makes for the author-function, except that the genre function accounts for all discursive activities, not just those endowed with a certain name or author-value. The genre function, as such, allows us to expand our field of inquiry to include the constitution of all discourses and the social commitments, practices, relations, identities, and silences implicated within them. Such an expanded view of genre will enable those who study and teach writing to account more fully for what writers do when they write, why they do it, and what happens to them as a result. In order to make the case for how genres function as sites of action, I will first turn to literary studies to examine how the genre function is at work organizing and generating literary practices and relations in a way that will later serve as a basis for examining how, in much the same manner, genres function to organize and generate everyday social practices and relations, including how processes of textual invention locate all writers within these practices and relations.

## GENRE AS SITE OF LITERARY ACTION

The relationship between genre and text has historically been and still remains an uneasy one in literary studies, with most scholars subordinating genre to an a posteriori classificatory status that privileges the autonomy of the text and its author. In such a configuration, genre is treated at best as a category, a transparent lens for looking at and organizing texts that presumably function independently of it, and at worst as an imposition on the text and its author's indeterminacy.[4] The genre function, however, elevates genre from a transparent category to a site of action. A number of literary scholars have recognized genres as such sites of action, and it is to their work that we will now look in order to see how genres frame the ideological and material conditions within which literary writers, texts, and their activities and relations function. As I will argue, such scholarship exposes the constitutive nature of genres in ways that complement and augment the work of rhetorical genre scholars. But because this work in literary genre theory tends to confine the function of genre only to literary actions and relations, we ultimately need to go beyond literary genre theory, as I will do in the next section, to see how genres constitute a wider range of social activities. First, though, I will examine how genres function as sites of literary action.

Heather Dubrow begins her 1982 survey of literary genre theory by asking readers to consider the following paragraph:

> The clock on the mantelpiece said ten thirty, but someone had suggested recently that the clock was wrong. As the figure of the dead woman lay on the bed in the front room, a no less silent figure glided rapidly from the house. The only sounds to be heard were the ticking of that clock and the loud wailing of an infant. (1)

How, Dubrow asks, do we make sense of this piece of discourse? What characteristics should we pay attention to as significant about it? What state of mind need we assume to interpret the action it describes? The relevance of these questions, Dubrow claims, points to the significance of genre in helping readers delimit and interpret discourse. For example, knowing that the paragraph appears in a novel with the title *Murder at Marplethorpe*, readers can begin to make certain interpretive decisions as to the value and meaning of specific images, images which become symbolic and material when readers recognize that the novel they are reading belongs to the genre of detective fiction. The inaccuracy of the clock and the fact that the woman lies dead in the front room become important clues when we know what genre we are reading. The figure gliding away assumes a particular subject position within the discourse, the subject position of suspect. If, Dubrow continues, the title of the novel was not *Murder at Marplethorpe* but rather *The Personal History of David Marplethorpe*, then the way we encounter the same text changes. Reading the novel as a *Bildungsroman*, we will place a different significance on the dead body or the fact that the clock is inaccurate. Certainly, we will be less likely to look for a suspect. That is, we will not be reading with "detective eyes" as we would if we were reading detective fiction. The crying baby, as Dubrow suggests, will also take on more relevance, perhaps being the very David Marplethorpe whose life's story we are about to read.

Dubrow's example is significant for what it reveals about what I am calling the genre function. Not only does the genre function in this case constitute how we read certain elements within the discourse, allowing us to occupy certain interpretive frames as readers of the discourse, but it also constitutes the roles and relations we assign to the actors and events within the discourse. The actors in the discourse—the crying baby, the dead woman, the inaccurate clock, the gliding figure—all assume subject positions within and because of the genre. Genre thus coordinates both the actors involved, including the reader and the characters, as well as their actions in specific textured relations and orientations so that, for example, the figure who glides rapidly away from the house can either be recognized as in the act of escape or in the act of seeking help, depending on the genre. The type of action taking place within the text, then, is largely constituted by the genre in which the text functions, because genre frames the conditions—what John Austin in his theory of speech acts calls the "felicity conditions" (1962)—within which utterances become speech acts. The meaning of the utterances in the Marplethorpe paragraph, including the actions these utterances are performing, the roles of the characters doing the performing, and even the sequence and timing of the utterances, are all interpretable in relation to the contextual conditions maintained by the genre. These genre conditions allow readers to limit the potentially multiple actions sustained by the utterances to certain recognizable social actions. As Bazerman explains, "even though multiplicity of action remains [especially in literary texts], attribution of genre still helps to limit the domain and focus the character of the multiplicities offered by, or to be read out of, the text—that is, genre recognition usually limits interpretive flexibility" (1994a, 90). Suffice it to say, we recognize, interpret, and, in the spirit of reader-response theory, also construct (and deconstruct) the discourses we encounter using the genre function. Genres, in short, function as sites of action that locate readers in positions of interpretation.

In her work, Dubrow acknowledges the genre function when she explains, following E. D. Hirsch (1967), that genre acts like a social code of behavior established between the reader and author (1982, 2), a kind of "generic contract" (31) that stabilizes and enables interpretation. Such a recognition, echoed in the work of Beebee (1994), Cohen (1989), Perloff (1989), Threadgold (1989), and Todorov (1970), understands genre as a psychological concept rather than a classification system, a disposition a reader assumes in relation to a literary text. But genres not only establish a relationship between reader and text in what amounts to a psychological relationship; they also establish a relationship between texts in what amounts to a sociological relationship—a kind of literary culture within which readers, writers, and texts function.

In the Marplethorpe example, we have already discussed the way that genres function on a psychological level as conceptual frameworks for interpretation, helping readers construct what reading theorist Frank Smith calls "specifications" with which to predict, navigate, and interpret texts (1994). On a sociological level, genres function to create a literary culture within which texts are defined and operate in relation to one another. Sociology is the science of social relations, organization, and change, what Anthony Giddens calls the study of "human social activities" and the "conditions that make these activities possible" (1984, 2). Sociologists study how social life is enacted and organized, how social activity is defined and related to other social activity in space-time. In his book *Metaphors of Genre*, David Fishelov explores the connections between sociology and genre theory, explaining that the metaphor "genres are social institutions" is commonly used by literary scholars to explain genre (1993). Like social institutions, genres coordinate textual relations, organization, and change. In fact, like social institutions, genres also frame the conditions that make literary activity possible and even meaningful, the discursive sites within which readers and writers organize, define, and enact textured language practices and relations.

Following Northrop Frye in his *Anatomy of Criticism*, Fishelov describes genres as shaping and governing a specifically literary universe, so that genre theory becomes akin to the sociology of literary culture or what is more commonly understood as "poetics." As René Wellek and Austin Warren put it, literary genres are institutions in the same way as church, university, and state are institutions (1942, 226). Fredric Jameson similarly describes genres as "essentially literary institutions, or social contracts between a writer and a specific public, whose function is to specify the proper use of a particular cultural artifact" (1981, 106). Genres thus endow literary texts with a social identity in relation to other texts within this "universe of literature" (Todorov 1970, 8), constituting a literary text's "mode of being" in that universe. This genred universe organizes and generates practices of textual production, circulation, and interpretation.

As sociological concepts, one way that genres organize and generate literary activity is by establishing particular space-time configurations within which texts function. Käte Hamburger, for example, argues that each genre choreographs a particular orientation, especially a temporal orientation, so that, for instance, the "past tense in fiction does not suggest the past tense as we know it but rather a situation in the present; when we read 'John walked into the room,' we do not assume, as we would if we encountered the same preterite in another type of writing, that the action being described occurred prior to one in our world" (qtd. in Dubrow 1982, 103). Genres synchronize our perceptions of time. But they also synchronize how we spatially negotiate our way through time, as both readers and writers. Recall, for example, the Marplethorpe paragraph discussed earlier. If we read it as detective fiction, then we immediately begin to make certain space-time connections: the gliding figure and the dead woman assume a certain spatial-temporal relationship to one another as possible murder victim and suspect. That is, they assume a genre-mediated cause-effect relationship in terms of their spatial proximity and their temporal sequence. The gliding figure may simply be a gliding figure, peripheral to the plot. However, if we read the paragraph as detective fiction, then this figure's gliding away from the site of a dead body at this particular time and at this particular distance makes this figure a suspect and the dead body a victim. The actions of each actor, in other words, along with the inaccurate clock, combine together within the genre to form a genre-mediated socio-rhetorical orientation in which space and time are configured in a certain way in order to allow certain events and actions to take place. Bakhtin refers to this articulation of space and time as "chronotope," which Schryer adapts to genre theory by positing that "every genre expresses space/time relations that reflect current social beliefs regarding the placement of human individuals in space and time and the kind of action permitted within that time/space" (1999, 83). Genres are discursive articulations of the chronotope.[5]

As conceived by the aforementioned scholars in literary studies, literary genres play a significant role in the "sociological" constitution of literary culture by helping to identify the various roles that texts and their authors play within it and how these roles get performed within the space-time configurations it constructs. This is why genre theorists often define genre in terms of literary social institutions, institutions that enable and shape "human social activities" and the "conditions that make these activities possible" (Giddens 1984, 2). David Fishelov, for example, explains that as "a professor is expected to comply with certain patterns of action, and to interact with other role-players (e.g. students) according to the structure and functions of an educational institution . . . , a character in a comedy is expected to perform certain acts and to interact with other characters according to the structural principles of the literary 'institution' of comedy" (1993, 86). It is these "structural principles," which often function and are articulated at the level of genre, that make the activity at once possible and recognizable, socially and rhetorically. And just as social institutions coordinate institutional positions and relations, so genres coordinate genre positions and relations, both in terms of the subjects who participate within them and the writers and readers who produce and interpret them. Yet the problem here, as has been the case traditionally within literary genre theory, is that literary scholars limit genre positions and relations only to literary activities. For many such scholars, genres function only to help organize and generate a literary institution, in which various literary activities and identities are enacted.

We can go a long way toward understanding genres as sites within which individuals acquire, negotiate, and enact everyday language practices and relations if we identify genres not only as *analogical* to social institutions but as *actual* social institutions, constituting not just literary activity but social activity, not just literary textual relations but all textual relations, so that genres do not just constitute the literary scene in which literary actors (writers, readers, characters) and their texts function, but also constitute the social conditions in which the activities of all social participants are enacted. For example, to what extent is the university as a social institution mediated by its genres, including research articles, grants, syllabi, assignment prompts, lectures, student essays, course evaluations, oral exams, memos, and committee minutes, to name just a few? This is the question that theorists in rhetorical genre studies have been asking over the last twenty years, and it is the question that we will now begin to consider. Answering it will allow us to begin synthesizing the literary as well as the nonliterary ways that the genre function is at work in making all kinds of social practices, relations, and subject positions possible and meaningful within situated space-time configurations. Answering it will also set the stage for later chapters to examine how the genre function positions writers and their processes of invention within specific social and rhetorical sites of action, whether these writers are D. H. Lawrence, a social worker, or a student in a first-year writing course. Understanding how genres situate and help generate rhetorical and social activities will allow us in composition studies to acquire a richer understanding of the writer and invention.

## GENRE AS SITE OF SOCIAL ACTION

Not all literary scholars limit genre's jurisdiction only to the literary world.[6] In "The Problem of Speech Genres," Bakhtin argues that genres mediate all communicative activity, from novels to military commands to everyday short rejoinders (1986). In so doing, Bakhtin takes perhaps the most significant step toward a view of genre as social, not just literary, action. Defining speech genres as typified utterances existing within language spheres (60), Bakhtin claims that "we speak only in definite speech genres[;] that is, all our utterances have definite and relatively stable typical *forms of construction of the whole*" (79; Bakhtin's emphasis). Such generic forms of the utterance shape and enable what Bakhtin calls a speaker's "speech plan" or "speech will" (78). After all, Bakhtin quips, "the speaker is not the biblical Adam, dealing only with virgin and still unnamed objects, giving them names for the first time" (93). Instead, every speaker's utterance exists in a dialogical relationship with previous utterances and can be understood through that relationship. Speech genres function as sites for the articulation and exchange of utterances. Bakhtin explains:

> The speaker's speech will is manifested primarily in the *choice of a particular speech genre*. This choice is determined by the specific nature of the given sphere of speech communication. . . . And when the speaker's speech plan with all its individuality and subjectivity is applied and adapted to a chosen genre, it is shaped and developed within a certain generic form. Such genres exist above all in the great and multifarious sphere of everyday oral communication, including the most familiar and the most intimate. (78; Bakhtin's emphasis)

Genres, therefore, do not just constitute literary reality and its texts. They constitute all speech communication by becoming part of "our experiences and our consciousness together" and mediating the "dialogic reverberations" that make up communicative interaction (78, 94).

Individuals communicate by choosing (and being chosen by) a particular genre (or by combining genres) within a system of related genres in a given sphere of speech communication—what is popularly referred to in composition studies as a discourse community but more accurately depicted by Bazerman (1997a) and Russell (1997), following Cole and Engeström, as an "activity system."[7] Avoiding the abstraction and homogeneity often associated with the idea of discourse community, an activity system describes the complex, coordinated, ongoing, and often contradictory interactions of individuals within "systems of purposeful activity" (Russell 2002). These systems are mediated by a constellation of related, sometimes conflicting genres, what Devitt (1991) calls "genre sets" and Bazerman (1994a) calls "genre systems," which enact and organize these interactions. An individual's choice of genre, then, is based to a large extent on his or her participation in and knowledge of the sphere of communication and its related genres, although of course it is also possible for communicants to import and export genres from one sphere to another as they travel through the various systems of activity that make up their lives. Within their chosen genres, communicants assume certain genre-constituted positions and participate in certain language games while interacting with one another. Bakhtin refers to the participants within language games as "speech subjects" (1986, 72). The speech subject's "speech plan" is mediated by his or her chosen genre, as is his or her style. In addition, the speech subject's very conception of the addressee is mediated by genre, because each genre embodies its own typical conception of the addressee (Bakhtin, 98). In fact, at the level of diction the very word and its relation to other words are also mediated by speech genres: "In the genre the word acquires a particular typical expression. Genres correspond to typical situations of speech communication, typical themes, and, consequently, also to particular contacts between the meanings of words and actual concrete reality under certain typical circumstances" (Bakhtin, 87). Speech genres thus organize and generate the very communicative conditions within which speech subjects—both speakers and addressees—interact, in the same way that literary genres constitute the literary contexts within which literary subjects—writers, readers, and characters—interact.[8]

## Trajectories of Inquiry: Genre and Register

In applied linguistics, the site of this dialectical relation between language and its situations of use is often defined as "register," the "conceptual framework for representing the social context as the semiotic environment in which people exchange meanings" (Halliday 1978, 110). The concepts of register and genre are closely related, but because this relationship is not always clear (some scholars see them as interchangeable; some see them as hierarchically distinguished, with either genre or register as the higher order concept; and some see them as different in value, with either genre or register as more useful to a systematic study of language), it is worthwhile briefly to examine the relationship between the two, especially since such an examination will contribute to an understanding of how genres organize and generate the conditions of discursive production in which writers and writing take place.

In his functional approach to language, articulated in *Language as Social Semiotic*, M. A. K. Halliday (1978) describes how "the network of meanings" that constitute any culture, what he calls the "social semiotic" (100), is to a large extent encoded in and maintained by its semantic system, which represents a culture's "meaning potential" (13). As such, "the construal of reality [social semiotic] is inseparable from the construal of the semantic system in which the reality is encoded. In this sense, language is a shared meaning potential, at once both a part of experience and an intersubjective interpretation of experience" (1–2). This is why, as Halliday insists, language is a form of socialization, playing a role in how individuals become socialized within formations of culture he calls "contexts of situation."

Language is functional not only because it encodes and embodies the social semiotic but also because it helps enact the social semiotic. Language, therefore, makes social reality recognizable and enables individuals to experience it, others, and themselves within it. Halliday explains: "By their everyday acts of meaning [their semantic activities], people act out the social structure, affirming their own statuses and roles, and establishing and transmitting the shared systems of value and of knowledge" (2). The semantic system, representing what Halliday calls a culture's "meaning potential," in turn constitutes its individuals' "behaviour potential," which characterizes individuals' actions and interactions within a particular social semiotic. The semiotic system, which is social in nature, becomes cognitively internalized as a system of behavior when it is manifested in the semantic system, so that we internalize and enact culture as we learn and use language. The semantic potential (what a communicator can do or mean within social reality) constitutes the "actualized potential" (what a communicator does or means within social reality) (40).

Halliday explains that contexts of situation are not isolated and unique, but often reoccur as "situation types," a set of typified semiotic and semantic relations that make up "a scenario . . . of persons and actions and events from which the things which are said derive their meaning" (28–30). Examples of situation types include "players instructing novice in a game," "mother reading bedtime story to a child," "customers ordering goods over the phone" (29). Because contexts of situation reoccur as situation types, those who participate in these situations develop typified ways of acting and interacting within them. As these situation types become conventionalized over time, they begin to "specify the semantic configurations that the speaker will typically fashion" (110).

Halliday refers to this typified social and semantic scenario as "register." Register is "the clustering of semantic features according to situation types" (68), a situated and typified semantic system which describes the activities of communicators, including their contexts and their means of communication, within a particular type of situation. Register assigns a situation type with particular syntactic and lexicogrammatic properties, becoming a linguistic realization of a situation type. As a framework within which a situation type is linguistically realized, register describes what actually takes place communicatively (the "field"), who is taking part (the "tenor"), and what role language is playing (the "mode"). For example, the "field" of discourse represents the setting in which language occurs; that is, the system of activity within a particular setting. The "tenor" of discourse represents the relation between participants—their interactions—within the discourse. And the "mode" of discourse represents the channel or wavelength of communication adopted by the participants (33). All three levels interact in particular and fairly typified ways within register. When linguists identify a "scientific register," then, they not only describe a style of language, but also the set of words, structural choices, and interactional patterns associated with scientific contexts.

Halliday locates genre as a mode or conduit of communication, one of the textual and linguistic means available within register that helps communicants realize the situation type. Functioning at the level of *mode*, within the field, tenor, and mode complex, genre represents the vehicle through which communicants interact within a situation type. In Halliday's model, genres are thus relegated to typified tools communicants use within registers to enact and interact within a particular type of situation. It is this situation, Halliday explains, "that generates the semiotic tensions and the rhetorical styles and genres that express them" (113). Yet, as we have been discussing so far, genres perform more than just an expressive function; they do not simply describe how participants typically communicate in typified situations. Rather, genres function in relation to other genres as typified sites of action that position their users within situated motives for action, language practices, and social relations and activities. And so, I propose to assign genres more of a constitutive role in Halliday's theory of language, imagining them as bounded discursive sites for the organization and realization of situation types, including the complex relations of field, tenor, and mode that take place within situation types.[9]

Elevating genre study as a method of inquiry over register not only allows us to identify and examine specific ideological, semantic, and lexicogrammatic configurations and activities within situation types, but it also allows us to interrogate the very nature of situation types. The study of register generally assumes a situation type as a precondition of language use and then goes on to describe that language use. Rhetorical genre study tends to offer genre as a location for the production and articulation of situation types. Part of the action genres accomplish, through their use, is the reproduction of the situations that require their use. As such, genre theory provides what might be called a "thicker" description of the textured, situated activities that reflect and generate complex forms of social organization. And so, although register is valuable for identifying and describing the language interactions within recurrent situations, it seems pitched at too abstract a level to help account for the specific activities and relations that comprise situation types. Within the same situation type, for example, more than one genre is often at work, and, as I will argue in more detail in chapters 4 and 5, each genre within a situation type constitutes its own situated register—that is, its own system of activity, its own subject positions as well as relations between these positions, and its own rhetorical and formal features.

Each genre, I argue, organizes and generates its own field, tenor, and mode complex—its own site of action—in relation to other genres within a larger sphere of action or "activity system." The genres that form this constellation function together to coordinate the dynamic relations that make up the larger activity systems. Within such systems, genres not only constitute particular participant positions and language practices; they also regulate how participants recognize and interact with one another. As such, any typified social activity is mediated by a range of genres, each of which frames its own situated genre identities and actions, including motives and intentions, as well as relations. This notion of situation type as one resulting from and mediated by a set of genres can be clarified if we look at an example.

If we take a situation type, say "teacher instructing students in a classroom," we recognize that there cannot be only one register at work within it. This situation type is much too dynamic—actualized by a range of shifting, even conflicting, situational activities, participant relations, and rhetorical styles and goals—to be embodied by a single register. What is at work within the situation type is a system of related genred sites of action that constitute what we recognize as this overall situation type. For instance, the lecture represents one genre which constitutes a particular field (literally the physical configuration of the room, with teacher in front, students facing teacher in rows, etc.), tenor (the way students raise their hands and wait for signals from the teacher to ask questions, and the power dynamic this sets up), and mode (how the teacher organizes the lecture itself, the question-answer nature of the dialogue, and so on). But it is not the only genre. Others include the assignment prompt, which in turn constitutes a different field, tenor, and mode; the student papers; the teacher's comments on the students' papers; the syllabus; the course description; and so on. Each of these genres organizes and generates a particular site of action which both students and teachers come to recognize and which in turn shapes and enables their various positions, activities, and relations within the situation type (see chapter 5 for more on the classroom as a genre-mediated environment).

Halliday writes that "reality consists of meanings" (139). Genres do not just express or help communicate these a priori meanings as part of register; rather, genres organize and generate these meanings. As such, genres are not merely classification systems or innocent communicative tools; genres are socially constructed, ongoing cognitive and rhetorical sites—symbiotically maintained rhetorical ecosystems, if you will—within which communicants enact and reproduce specific situations, actions, relations, and identities. As individuals make their way through culture, they function within various and at times conflicting genred spaces, spaces that reposition them in specific relations to others through the use of specific language exchanges as well as frame the ways they recognize and enact their language practices, activities, and themselves.

GENRE AND THE ENACTMENT OF SOCIAL MOTIVES

In later chapters, we will consider how writers' rhetorical inventions, including their motives and intentions to invent, take place within and against the very genred sites of action that construct their subject positions and social relations. Here, though, I would like to conclude this chapter by examining how, as sites of action, genres maintain the desires that writers acquire, negotiate, and articulate—how, that is, genres locate writers in relation to desires that inform the choices they make when they begin to write.

Sociologist Anthony Giddens argues that human activity—including motive, intention, and agency—is constituted by, enacted within, and helps reproduce social systems. Giddens explains: "Human social activities . . . are recursive. That is to say, they are not brought into being by social actors but continually recreated by them via the very means whereby they express themselves as actors. In and through their activities agents reproduce the conditions that make these activities possible" (1984, 2). Giddens describes this ecological process as the "duality of structure," which is based on the theory "that the rules and resources drawn upon in the production and reproduction of social action are at the same time the means of system reproduction" (19). I will address Giddens's theory of structuration in greater detail in chapter 4. For now, let me just note that human actors, in their social practices, reproduce the very social conditions that in turn make their actions necessary, possible, and recognizable, so that their actions maintain and enact the very conditions that consequently call for these actions.

Giddens's theory of structuration, echoing Raymond Williams's (1981) Marxist formulation of the dynamic correspondence between the *base* (productive forces) and *superstructure* (cultural practices), has much to offer genre studies. Carolyn Miller (1994), for one, has explored the connections by arguing that genres, as typified socio-rhetorical sites of action, play a mediating role in enabling their users to reproduce the very conditions of production within which they in turn function.[10] Miller writes: "The rules and resources of a genre provide reproducible speaker and addressee roles, social typifications of recurrent social needs or exigencies, topical structures (or 'moves' and 'steps'), and ways of indexing an event to material conditions, turning them into constraints and resources" (1994, 71). But how do genres do this? How do they maintain the desires that they help to fulfill?

We function within genre-constituted conditions that we socially and rhetorically sustain in our practices because, as Miller has argued (1984), genre is recursively and inseparably linked to the concept of exigence, defined as a situation or event that we recognize as requiring immediate attention or response. Exigencies compel us to respond and/or act. Yet our compulsions to act are not as intuitive or unmediated as we might think. On a physiological level, of course, we certainly do respond instinctively, as when we quickly withdraw our hand after touching a hot stove. But exigence, as Miller explains, is not instinctive in the same way. Rather, exigence is learned behavior, a learned recognition of significance that informs why and how we learn to respond in and to various situations. In our social interactions, all sorts of conventions mediate how we recognize exigencies as social motives to act. Genres are examples of such mediating conventions. As cultural artifacts, they embody exigencies, and in using genres, we enact and reinforce these exigencies as recognizable, meaningful, consequential actions.

An example will help clarify how genres predispose us to act and/or respond in certain ways by rhetorically framing how we conceptualize certain situations as social motives. Like many other events, death is a physical and social reality in our world, one that calls for various and often culturally idiosyncratic reactions. At some basic level, our response to death is certainly instinctive, perhaps even biological, but at the ideological level in which we function as social beings, our response to death is mediated by a range of social and rhetorical conventions, including genres, each of which constitutes death as a slightly different exigency recognized as a particular social motive requiring a particular type of immediate attention or response. The various ways in which individuals recognize, experience, and respond to death, therefore, become informed by the genres available to them and those they "choose" to use.

As a situation type, the "response to death" is represented and realized by a variety of genres in contemporary Western culture, each of which constitutes it as a specific exigency, calling for a particular kind of response to fill a particular social need. So each genre constitutes its own site of action within which death takes on a particular social meaning and becomes treated as a particular social action (field), within which those involved take on particular social roles and relate to one another in particular ways (tenor), and within which certain rhetorical strategies and styles are used (mode). In our culture, for example, we have elegies, eulogies, obituaries, epitaphs, requiems, even greeting cards, just to name a few. Each of these socially sanctioned and typified rhetorical responses is not just a form or a tool we use to express our feelings about death as an a priori exigency; instead, each comes to constitute one of the various, sometimes conflicting ways we make sense of and treat death in our culture by transforming it into a specific social motive. The obituary and the elegy, for instance, rhetorically respond to death differently because each genre represents death as a slightly different exigency, serving a different social motive and requiring a different type of immediate attention and remedy. Thus, the genres we have available to us are integral to the ways we construct, respond to, and make sense of recurring situations, even when these situations revolve around the same physical event. At the same time, genres are related to the subject positions we assume, the language practices we enact, as well as the relations we establish between ourselves and others within these situations.

We recognize obituaries, for example, as notices of a person's death, usually accompanied by a short biographical account. They serve to notify the general public, and so do not play as direct a role as, say, the eulogy does in helping those who are grieving deal with their loss. The purpose of the obituary, then, is not so much to console those closest to the deceased or to help them maintain a sense of continuity in the face of loss, but to ascribe the deceased with a social identity and value, one that is recognizable to others within the community. So the obituary's purpose is not, like the eulogy, to assess and praise the meaning of the deceased's life and death; rather, it is to make the deceased's life publicly recognizable, perhaps even to celebrate the value of the individual-as-citizen. Rhetorically, therefore, the obituary often begins with an announcement of death, often without mention of the cause, and a notice of where the funeral services will be held. What is most telling about the obituary, though, is how it biographically represents the deceased. Unlike the eulogy, in which the deceased's personal accomplishents, desires, even disappointments are celebrated, the obituary describes the deceased's life in terms of its social value: who the deceased's parents are, who his or her spouse(s) and children are, where the deceased was born, lived, and died, what jobs the deceased held over the span of his or her life, what organizations and clubs the deceased belonged to, and so on. In other words, the obituary narrates a certain public identity for the deceased, one that makes him or her recognizable to the general public in terms familiar to them: as a fellow citizen. As a genre, then, the obituary constitutes death as an exigence that motivates us to reaffirm, using the occasion of someone's death, the public worth of that individual. The obituary positions the deceased as a public citizen, whose life is told in terms of the public institutions in which he or she participated. In short, the obituary constitutes death as a different kind of exigency endowed with a different social motive that requires a different rhetorical action, a different relation among the participants, and different social roles than does the eulogy or other related genres.

Carolyn Miller argues that because "situations are social constructs that are the result, not of 'perception,' but of definition," the very idea of recurrence is socially defined and constructed (1984, 156). What we recognize and experience as recurring is the result of our construing and treating it as such. Moreover, the way we recognize a recurring situation as requiring a certain immediate attention or remedy (in short, an exigence) is also socially defined. Over time, a recursive relationship results, in which our typified responses to a situation in turn lead to its recurrence. As Giddens would put it, we reproduce a situation as we act within and in response to it. In all this, exigence plays a key role, at once shaping how we socially recognize a situation and helping us rhetorically enact it. As Miller explains, "exigence is a form of social knowledge—a mutual construing of objects, events, interests, and purposes that not only links them but also makes them what they are: an objectified social need" (157). Exigence becomes part of the way we conceptualize and experience a situation by endowing it with social meaning—meaning that shapes how individuals act within the situation. This dynamic process is bound up in and made possible by genre. Exigence, as such, is not only a form of social knowledge but also specifically a form of *genre* knowledge. We rhetorically recognize, respond to, and potentially change exigence through genres, because genres are how we socially construct situations by defining and treating them as particular social motives.

We recognize this phenomenon when we look at the genre of the greeting card. The greeting card may have emerged as a response to recurring physical and social exigencies (birth of loved ones, marriage, and so on), but the greeting card also serves to transform these exigencies into social motives by endowing them with a certain social significance that in turn sanctions them as deserving of a greeting card, a typified rhetorical action. Today we see the extent to which the greeting card as a genre constructs the very recurring exigencies to which it responds in such examples as the "secretaries' day card," the "bosses' day card," the "grandparents' day card," etc. The greeting card, then, like the obituary (and like all genres, literary and nonliterary), becomes part of its users' "regularized social relations, communicative landscape, and cognitive organization" (Bazerman 1997b, 22). Within this genre environment, writers and other communicants "acquire and strategically deploy genre knowledge," which refers to situated cognition (Berkenkotter and Huckin 1995, 3); assume genre identities; and, as we saw earlier, reproduce the very recurrence that they come to recognize as a situation type. Genre, therefore, is not merely a rhetorical tool that comes after the semiotic fact; it is itself the semiotic fact—the site of "social and ideological action" (Schryer 1994, 107) in which social motives are maintained and enacted.[11]

Because genres are one of the ways that exigencies are transformed into social motives—that is, because genres constitute both our need to respond and the way in which we do so—I argue that genres are sites which enable and shape communicative action by first staging the social situation in which communication takes place and then motivating the way communicants rhetorically act within it, including the positions they assume and the relations they enact. It is how and why these genre-constituted positions, relations, commitments, and practices affect the choices writers make when they begin to write that will be the focus of the remainder of the book.

## SUMMARY

This book is based on the premise that genres function as sites of action in which writers acquire, articulate, and potentially resist motives to act. It conceives of genre as operating on both an ideological and a material level—both a disposition and its articulation. Fundamental to this understanding is the notion that genre is a social motive and a rhetorical instantiation of that motive. Genre *is* what it allows us to do, the potential that makes the actual possible, the concept and its practice, the "con-" and the "-text" at the same time. As such, genre allows us to study the social situation and the rhetorical action as they are at work on one another, reinforcing and reproducing one another. This is why genre is both social and rhetorical, the articulation and effect of what we do and the reason and means for why we do it.

As we write various texts, then, we rhetorically enact and reproduce the desires that prompted them. This recursive process is what genre *is*. And as we rhetorically enact and reproduce these desires, we also rhetorically enact, reproduce, and potentially resist and/or transform the social activities, the roles, and the relations that are embedded in these desires. It is the genred positions, commitments, and relations that writers assume, enact, and sometimes resist within certain situations that most interest me. In particular, I am interested in the way these positions, commitments, and relations inform the choices writers make during the scene of invention. As we make our way from day to day and from situation to situation, we assume various and at times even conflicting genre identities, identities which are certainly informed by our gender, our sexual orientation, our class, our race, our ethnicity, our personal history, our immediate context, and our genetics. In chapter 4, we will consider how these factors affect genre identity formation and potential transformation. Yet, as we will also see, there is always the ideology of genre at work, an ideology with which we have to contend. Some genres invite more resistance than others. Literary genres, for example, are more self-conscious than most nonliterary genres. As Thomas Beebee argues, literary writers often resist their generic categorizations even as they exist within them, so that they self-consciously position themselves on the margins of different genres: "the meaning of a literary text can depend on the play of differences between its genres" (1994, 250). Other, more "rhetorical," genres are less pliable but just as transformable. No matter our motives, whether to resist or conform to social and rhetorical conventions, the choices we make as writers before and when we begin to write are always mediated by genres. Invention takes place within genres, and can be a site of conformity and/or resistance.

For example, there are the cases in which women poets have sought to invent differently by subverting male-dominated genres such as the elegy. Peter Sacks, for instance, has argued that the elegy performs what Freud terms the "work of mourning," and so "each elegy is to be regarded . . . as a work, both in the commonly accepted meaning of a product and in the more dynamic sense of the working through of an impulse or experience" (1985, 1). The elegy as a genre, just like the obituary as a genre, shapes and enables how we as a culture "work through" our experiences with death, albeit in different ways. According to Sacks, the elegy helps us work through our mourning in its very poetic movements, representing, as such, a rhetorical journey in which our loss becomes compensated by the elegy itself (6). Intended to overcome grief, this compensatory function of the elegy, Allison Giffen explains, represents male desire for

Oedipal resolution (1997, 121). In a very interesting twist, how-ever, Giffen claims that early American women poets strategi-cally appropriated the elegy for their own ends. Because grief was one of the few socially permissible emotions a woman could express poetically, early American women poets began to write elegies at an unprecedented rate, so much so that "the elegiac voice emerges as one of the most distinctive features of the poet-ess" (118). But they subverted the elegy by using it to sustain grief rather than to overcome it—to resist resolution and to maintain attachment with the lost beloved rather than to seek poetic compensation. The reason for this is not so much that these women poets had more of an inherent or intuitive store of grief; rather, by sustaining grief, Giffen explains, these women poets could continue to write: "to cease grieving, would mean to give up her poetry" (119). So these women poets adopted an elegiac identity while partly undermining the social purpose of the elegy, so that, within the "marginalized site of grief, [these poets are] able to articulate desire for a lost love object and thus define [themselves] as speaking subject[s]" (118). Such an elegy-mediated identity gave these poets a voice, but also defined them as grieving subjects, "characterized as saccharine, pious, and maudlin" (118). As much as gender played a role in how these women poets positioned themselves within the genre, ultimately the elegy allowed them to "define [themselves] as speaking subject[s]" only by *defining them* as speaking subjects. Even resistance to genre still leaves us functioning within genre.

What happens to writers when they write? This is, in its most general form, the question this book seeks to answer. What motivates the choices writers make before and as they begin to write? What happens to writers as they move from one genre to the next? In what way is a writer's subject position shaped by the genre in which he or she writes? How are a writer's intentions shaped by the genre in which he or she writes? How do writers transform genres as they work within them? And, as a result, to what extent does invention involve writers in the process of acquiring and articulating a rhetorical subjectivity within genre rather than the process of expressing self-possessed motives? The notion that genres are sites of action, as I have examined it in this chapter, suggests that a writer's ways of (re)cognizing—that is, both identifying and knowing—and carrying out his or her purpose, subject matter, and even intentions is organized and generated by the genres in which he or she writes. We can learn a great deal about how and why writers invent by analyzing how writers get positioned within these genred sites of action. We can also, I will argue, demystify invention by teaching students how to make these sites of action visible to themselves in a way that allows them to participate more consciously and critically at the intersection between the acquisition and articulation of motives where agency and beginnings take place.

# 3
## INVENTING THE WRITER IN COMPOSITION STUDIES

The first stage [of composing], the finding of material by thought or observation, is the fundamental and inclusive office of invention. . . . Yet this is, of all processes, the one least to be invaded by the rules of the textbook. It is a work so individual, so dependent on the particular aptitude and direction of the writer's mind, that each one must be left for the most part to find his way alone, according to the impulse that is in him.

JOHN GENUNG, "The Study of Rhetoric in the College Course"

Genres, in-so-far as they identify a repertoire of possible actions that may be taken in a set of circumstances, identify the possible intentions one may have. Thus they embody the range of social intentions toward which one may orient one's energies.

CHARLES BAZERMAN, "Systems of Genres and the Enactment of Social Intentions"

The above observations by Genung and Bazerman, made more than a century apart, represent two possible ways of imagining the writer-as-agent in composition. Genung locates agency within the writer, whose self-motivated, private intentions guide his or her processes of invention. Bazerman locates agency within a larger sphere of social motives, which orients and generates a writer's intentions to act. In both cases, Genung and Bazerman acknowledge that intention "belongs" to the writer and shapes how he or she begins to write, but they present different visions of where intentions come from and how and why they are acquired, leading to questions about the nature of agency and where it resides. That writers "have" intentions and that writers are the most palpable agents of invention is not under dispute.

Under dispute, rather, is how writers come to have intentions in the first place. And here we return to the question of motive that we began to address in the previous chapter, namely, what is involved when we say what writers are doing and why they are doing it? Writers, of course, are the ones who do the writing; they are the most obvious and immediate agents of their writing, the ones who transform intentions into words and actions as they invent their texts. But to designate and treat writers as the sole agents of invention because they are its most visible agents, as is largely still the case in composition pedagogy (Howard 1999, 57, 163), is to overlook the less obvious but just as significant factors that are at work on the writer, factors that shape writers' intentions and motivate the choices they make as agents.[1] As I will describe at the end of this chapter, genre theory helps us extend the sphere of agency in the study and teaching of writing to include not only what writers do when they write, but what happens to writers that makes them do what they do. Extending the sphere of agency in this way allows us to explore Kenneth Burke's expression "the motivation to act" in the fullness of its complexity, as a process of simultaneously acting and being acted upon. Such a formulation recognizes the writer as a "double agent," one who is both an agent *of* his or her desires and actions and an agent *on behalf of* already existing desires and actions. Invention occurs at the intersection of this dialectic between the social and the individual (which includes what Marshall Alcorn describes as the relation between libidinal attachments and ideological structures [2002, 23]) where agency is acquired, negotiated, resisted, and deployed. As they invent, writers participate in this agency, but they are not its sole agents.

Generally speaking, process-based research and pedagogy in composition studies have privileged the writer as the primary agent of invention. Toward that end, scholars and teachers of writing have developed valuable methods of encouraging writers, alone and in collaboration with others, to discover, organize, construct, reconstruct, and reflect on their ideas and writing in ways that acknowledge and manage their agency as writers. As valuable as such work has been and continues to be, however, it leaves us with a partial understanding of the agency at work when writers write, an understanding that imagines the writer as the point of departure for writing. Even when teachers acknowledge the social presence of writing by creating a space for and encouraging writers to collaborate with others, this social participation still mainly identifies and serves writers as the primary agents of writing, who invent privately and *then* subject the work of their invention to the influences of others (see Lunsford and Ede 1994, 431; and Howard 1999, 36–39). This partial notion of agency not only informs the teaching of invention, but, as I will argue in the final chapter, it also limits the teaching of writing in ways that ultimately threaten the place and purpose of post-secondary writing instruction. Yet it remains the prevailing notion, despite the work of composition scholars who have challenged it and offered in its place evidence of the thoroughly social nature of invention and authorship (see, for example, LeFevre 1987, Brodkey 1987, S. Miller 1989, Cooper 1989, Ede and Lunsford 1990, Faigley 1992, Lunsford and Ede 1994, and Howard 1999).

In this chapter, I investigate how and why process-based methodologies in composition came to privilege such a partial view of the writer and invention, a view that "invents" the writer as the primary site and agent of writing. At the end of the chapter and in the remainder of the book, I will examine what it would mean for the study and teaching of invention if we located intentions within a larger sphere of agency that includes not only the writer as agent but also the social and rhetorical conditions, namely genres, which participate in this agency and in which the writer and writing take place. Recasting invention in this way challenges us to reconsider entrenched assumptions about the writer and what it means to write in ways that will contribute, I hope, a richer, more pedagogically useful understanding of both.

## THE PROCESS MOVEMENT IN COMPOSITION: RECLAIMING INVENTION

In order to uncover general assumptions about the writer and invention in composition, we need to locate these assumptions in the context of the process movement in which they emerged.

The writing process movement in composition studies, as is well known, developed in the 1960s and 1970s as a rejection of traditional, product-driven, rules-based writing instruction. And with its popularization in the years since, the process movement has helped legitimize composition as a theoretical and professional academic discipline by giving those involved in it something to study in addition to something to teach, namely students' composing processes (Crowley 1998, 191; see also Harris 1997 and S. Miller 1991). Such an emphasis on the process rather than the product of writing—really a shift in attention from textual *product* to textual *production*—resulted in a shift in focus away from arrangement and correctness (this is what a finished text should look like) and back to invention (this is how a finished text comes to exist), thereby encouraging composition scholars to investigate the archeology of textual production right down to its beginnings in the writer's mind, the very realm, Genung had explained a half century earlier, that textbooks and teachers cannot invade. Influenced by work in cognitive psychology and creativity theory, early studies of writing processes such as Janet Emig's (1971) and Sondra Perl's (1979) demonstrated that writing is not simply the product of already formulated thought, but rather the process of working through thought, the process, as Perl explains, of seeing "in our words a further structuring of the sense we began with and . . . [recognizing] that in those words we have discovered something new about ourselves and our topic" (1988, 117). This attention to process revealed and provided access to an entire cognitive geography behind textual production, a geography that led many process theorists once again to inquire, after a period of neglect, into the nature of invention.

In shifting the balance of inquiry from the product to its production, advocates of process pedagogy inaugurated a veritable renaissance in rhetorical invention. "It is no accident," Richard Young wrote in 1978, "that the gradual shift in attention among rhetoricians from composed product to the composing process is occurring at the same time as the reemergence of invention as a rhetorical discipline" (33). Renewed interest in invention, Young explains, was heavily influenced by classical rhetoric, work in linguistics, and research in mid-twentieth century cognitive psychology and creativity theory. These different influences led to different and competing trajectories of inquiry into invention during the '60s and '70s, including Corbett's use of the classical topoi, Young, Becker, and Pike's development of tagmemic rhetoric, and Rohman and Wlecke's work on prewriting (Young 1978; for a more detailed account of competing theories of invention, see Lauer 1984). These influences also led to different heuristic procedures for teaching invention. Classical rhetoric contributed the topics, which provided rhetors with strategies for finding arguments; tagmemic rhetoric, developing from work in linguistics, provided strategies for inquiring into a problem from various perspectives and then formulating and solving it; and prewriting, growing out of work in creativity theory and developmental psychology, provided strategies to stimulate the discovery of ideas within writers through the use of journaling, meditation, and thinking-via-association. While classical and tagmemic rhetoric located invention for the most part externally in relation to an audience, argument, or problem, prewriting located invention introspectively in relation to the writer. Yet despite their different orientations, these theories and practices of invention did what current-traditional rhetoric had not done—they rendered invention accessible to inquiry, rendered it, that is, codifiable and teachable.

Rohman's and Wlecke's work on prewriting, referencing and reinforcing entrenched post-Enlightenment concepts of authorship, has had the most enduring influence on process-based pedagogies of invention. To this day, composition teachers and textbooks frequently refer to invention as prewriting and promote introspective heuristics such as freewriting, mapping, clustering, and brainstorming to help students discover and generate subject matter about which they will consequently write. These heuristics rightfully acknowledge and endorse writers as agents of their invention, the ones who access, develop, and articulate (with or without the collaboration of others) desires and intentions. But alone, these heuristics do not account for the complex relations of agency in which writers participate during invention. Their use overlooks, for example, the extent to which invention situates writers within what I, following Schryer (1994) and Bazerman (2002), described in chapter 2 as genred sites of action in which writers acquire, negotiate, and articulate desires and intentions. Ironically, for example, teachers and textbooks frequently overlook the fact that heuristics such as freewriting, brainstorming, and clustering, far from "free," are themselves discursive and ideological sites of action, genres that position writers within situated commitments, relations, and subjectivities.[2] By texturing cognition in specific ways (both in the sense of locating cognition within textual formations and in the sense of organizing or "texturing" cognition), these genres not only enable writers to acquire and articulate certain kinds of desires, but they also enable writers to participate in as well as potentially resist the discursive relations and activities bound up in and deployed through these desires. Agency gets enacted within these genred sites of action, but, again, writers are not its only agents. When composition pedagogies position writers as the primary or originating agents of invention, they deny writers access to the agency in which they necessarily participate. In so doing, such pedagogies perpetuate what Howard, following LeFevre (1987), Crowley (1990), and Lunsford and Ede (1994), calls the "normative model of the inspired, autonomous author [which] so pervades contemporary composition pedagogy that it even informs models for classroom collaboration" (1999, 57). This model is symptomatic (in the psychoanalytical sense of the term) of the enduring attachments teachers have to the idea of invention as prewriting and of writers as its originating agents.

In reclaiming invention as a teachable subject, thus, the process movement shifted the focus of writing instruction from the text and toward the writer. This shift from text to writer resulted in the destabilization of the text, since the text became treated as an ongoing production rather than as a freestanding product. The text now had a history that could be traced to its writer's mind and analyzed through the processes of its production. The process movement, hence, rejected the modernist stability of the new critical literary text as something somehow already composed only to be interpreted and evaluated, and embraced a view of the text as something contingent, something that is always in the process of being composed. Yet, for all its challenges to the text as a fixed, stable, and final product, for all its emphasis on revision, open-endedness, and recursivity, the process movement remains a decidedly modernist practice when it comes to its preservation of the writer as the self-possessed, identifiable agent of invention.[3] The process movement has left composition studies with an archeology and even a psychology of texts, but it has not equally provided a sociology of texts that accounts as fully for their social and socializing presence, as recent work in post-process theory has argued (see Kent 1999).

As a result, process-based theories of writing continue to posit the writer as an "originating consciousness" from which invention begins (Crowley 1990, 16). Indeed, Karen Burke LeFevre reflects, "composition theory and pedagogy in nineteenth and twentieth century America have been founded on a Platonic view of invention, one which assumes that the individual possesses innate knowledge or mental structures that are the chief source of invention. According to this view, invention occurs largely through introspective self-examination" (1987, 11). What I find curious about this concept of the writer is not so much that it still dominates our cultural and pedagogical imaginary, but that it remains as an assumption still shared by both current-traditional *and* process pedagogies. In what follows, I would like to consider briefly why even more recent process-based theories and practices of invention, despite having rejected so much of the current-traditional practices that had informed their views, continue, as John Genung did in 1892, to view invention as "a work so individual, so dependent on the particular aptitude and direction of the writer's mind, that each one must be left for the most part to find his way alone, according to the impulse that is in him" (217).

## THE MORE THINGS CHANGE . . . : THE DEATH (AND REBIRTH) OF INVENTION

By the time Genung wrote those words in the late nineteenth century, invention had been pretty much exiled from the public realm of rhetoric and relegated to the private workings of the writer's mind. So much so, in fact, that by the middle of the nineteenth century most composition and rhetoric textbooks no longer even bothered to deal with it in any substantial way. As Alexander Bain confidently explains in his popular textbook, *English Composition and Rhetoric* (first published in 1866), "The direct bearing of the Rhetorical act is, *of course*, not Invention, but Correctness; in other words, polish, elegance, or refinement" (1887,vii; my emphasis). The matter of fact way in which Bain makes this claim suggests how prevalent this assumption regarding rhetoric had become, but this assurance masks the fact that the assumption was at most only a hundred years old, largely a result, as I will explain in more detail shortly, of eighteenth century empiricism. For over two thousand years before that, invention was central to the rhetorical act.

Aristotle, as is well known, defined rhetoric as the art of discovering the available means of persuasion in any given situation. Invention, as "the canon of classical rhetoric through which arguments, or the substance of a message, are discovered or devised" (C. Miller 1980, 243), was central to this art. As Scott Consigny argues, "the art of rhetoric is thus a heuristic art, allowing the rhetor to discover real issues in indeterminate situations" (1994, 63). To assist rhetors in discovering the available means of persuasion, classical rhetoricians devised a series of topics (topoi) or commonplaces to serve as heuristics to invention. The topoi, as the etymology of the word suggests, were "places" rhetors could go to locate the available means of persuasion for a given situation. Aristotle, for example, distinguished between common and special topics. The former were invention strategies that could be used on any occasion—"depositories of general arguments that one could resort to when discussing virtually any subject"—and included definition, comparison, relationship, circumstance, and testimony (Corbett 1990, 97, 133). The latter were discourse-specific invention strategies "guiding the rhetor to subject matter as evidence for different rhetorical situations" (Lauer 1996, 725). In his *De Inventione*, Cicero extended Aristotle's topics as inventional techniques to include even more conceptual lines of discovering effective means of argumentation (Farrell 1996, 116). In their various manifestations, the topoi were publicly available to language users, quite literally, Sharon Crowley explains, "located in the participants' current or potential discourse" (1990, 68). As such, the topoi were part of the collected wisdom of a community, based on shared assumptions and communal knowledge, for locating one's discourse, including lines of reasoning, types of evidence, and appeals to audiences, within a social method of inquiry (Crowley 1990, 3, 68). To invent, to discover or formulate the available means of persuasion, a rhetor had to turn to these socially agreed upon topoi for guidance. Rhetors had to place themselves within these already existing rhetorical places.

Treating invention as an act so private as to be inaccessible and unteachable or, at its most extreme, as an act that does not even belong within the scope of rhetoric was very much a phenomenon that had its beginnings in eighteenth century empiricism—the birth of modernism. It had to do with a momentous shift in theories regarding the nature of knowledge, of epistemology—where knowledge comes from and how it is produced. "In classical epistemology," Crowley explains, "wise persons were those who had thought long and hard about the cultural assumptions that influenced their lives and those of other persons. In turn, their shared wisdom became part of communal knowledge. Knowledge itself was always changing its shape, depending on who was doing the knowing. Every act of knowing influenced the body of knowledge itself" (1990, 162). Classical epistemology thus proceeded deductively from a set of social assumptions, with rhetoric being a discursive means of engaging in these assumptions and participating in the communal actions upon which they are predicated (the enthymeme is a case in point). The topoi or commonplaces enabled rhetors to gain access to this social knowledge, making classical rhetoric, as Robert Connors explains, a "public discipline, devoted to examining and arguing questions that could be shared by all members of the polity" (1997, 298–99). Modern epistemology, however, privatized the locus of knowledge so that inquiry proceeded inductively from external parts derived from sense impressions to an internal whole derived through mental association.[4] Such a privatized economy not only shifted the trajectory of invention from an outwardly directed activity to an inwardly directed activity, thereby placing invention outside the realm of rhetoric and within the logical workings of the individual mind, but as Howard, following M. Rose, explains, it also identified the results of mental labor as the property of the individual that produced them (1999, 79–80).

Whereas classical epistemology saw rhetoric as a means of socially participating in the shared knowledge of the polis, eighteenth century epistemology literally saw rhetoric as an afterthought, a means not of inventing ideas but of arranging them logically and clearly so that they could be communicated (or miscommunicated) to others (see Berlin 1987; Connors 1981; Crowley 1990; C. Miller 1979; Murphy 1990). The shift from invention to arrangement as the central focus of modern rhetoric had far-reaching effects on the teaching of writing for almost the next two hundred years, not to be seriously challenged until the early 1960s with the renaissance of classical rhetoric and, as we discussed earlier, the emergence of the process movement. The history of this modern rhetoric, what came to be known as "current-traditional" rhetoric, and its impact on the teaching of writing is by now well known to scholars in composition and rhetoric, and it is not necessary for me to rehearse it here.[5] Instead, I would like to explore in more detail why this modernist emphasis on the individual mind as the locus of knowledge came to privatize the study and teaching of rhetorical invention to this day.

If one assumes that individuals accumulate knowledge empirically through experience, rational investigation, and research, and if one also assumes that reason is self-evident, then there is little need to teach invention since, on the one hand, writers either possess knowledge or they do not and, on the other hand, there is no need for writers to discover strategies for persuasion. Instead, the teaching of rhetoric involves helping the individual arrange already formulated ideas so that they can be communicated accurately to others. In his influential *Lectures on Rhetoric and Belles Lettres* (first published in 1783), for example, Hugh Blair rejected classical invention altogether by arguing that rational investigation, rather than rhetorical inquiry, would lead to the shaping of arguments (Crowley 1990, 11). "In a single stroke," Crowley claims, "Blair placed the entire process of invention beyond the province of rhetorical study, arguing that the art of rhetoric can only teach people how to manage the arguments they have discovered by other [more empirical] means" (11).

Such a privatized notion of invention held "the quality of an author's mind solely to account for the quality of his discursive intentions" (Crowley 1990, 54). After all, as Samuel Newman observed in his *Practical System of Rhetoric* (first published in 1827), "the store-house of the mind must be well filled; and [a rhetor] must have that command over his *treasures*, which will enable him to bring forward, whenever the occasion may require, what has here been accumulated for future use" (1838, 16–17; my emphasis). In this formulation, ideas and intentions not only reside pre-rhetorically within a writer's mind, but, as suggested by the word "treasures," they are also a form of capital that a writer owns. It is not surprising, then, that by 1892 John Genung can describe invention as an act so individual, "so dependent on the peculiar aptitude and direction of the writer's mind," that writers must be left to invent alone. Equally not surprising is the move, toward the latter part of the nineteenth century, to abandon the teaching of invention altogether, since invention was so introspective, so individual, that it could not be taught. A. S. Hill, the Boylston Chair of Rhetoric at Harvard from 1876 to 1904—the time during which some of the earliest first-year writing courses were being developed (see Berlin 1987)—placed invention out of the reach of rhetoric when he proclaimed in his extremely popular textbook, *Principles of Rhetoric and Their Amplification* (1878), that rhetoric "does not undertake to furnish a person with something to say"; it "shows how to convey from one mind to another the results of observation, discovery, or classification" (iv). It was in this context that the first-year writing course emerged as an institutional reality, a context that saw rhetoric as product replace rhetoric as production, signaling not only the privatization of invention, but also the diminishment of rhetoric as an epistemic process.

Today, our teaching of invention remains so invested in a private economy of the writer as a self-possessed agent that we forget that it was this very invention of the writer as self-possessed agent that led to the diminishment of rhetorical invention in the first place. So many of our contemporary perceptions of invention assume the writer as its starting point that the way we understand and teach invention today is premised on an epistemology that has well nigh destroyed it. Even by the 1960s when the process movement in composition studies tipped the rhetorical balance from product back to production and hence rescued invention by once again giving it a central role in the teaching of writing, it maintained the partial view of the writer as the primary agent of invention rather than as an agent who participates within a larger discursive and ideological agency. Yet whereas current-traditional rhetorics dismissed it as unteachable because inherent, process-based rhetorics recognized invention as generative (as the stage of the writing process in which writers construct knowledge rather than recall it), and developed a range of strategies for helping writers, alone or in collaboration with others, to *learn* through writing. In so doing, the process movement defined the writer's growth as the subject of writing instruction.

D. Gordon Rohman and Albert O. Wlecke's 1964 federally funded research project on "prewriting" reveals this focus on the writer's development as the subject matter of writing instruction. As Rohman defines it in his 1965 article, "Pre-Writing: The Stage of Discovery in the Writing Process," prewriting is all that happens before the point at which the "'writing idea' is ready for the words on the page" (1994, 41)— that is, before arrangement. Prewriting has been neglected, Rohman argues, because it exists "within the mind and [is] consequently hidden," yet it marks a formative stage in the writing process (42). It is formative because it shapes thinking, which Rohman describes as

> that activity of mind which brings forth and develops ideas, plans, designs, not merely the entrance of an idea into one's mind; an active, not a passive enlistment in the "cause" of an idea; conceiving, which includes consecutive logical thinking but much more besides; essentially the imposition of pattern upon experience. (41)

Here we recognize many of the assumptions that guide the process movement, the most significant of which is that far from being simple mental reflections of the external world, our ideas actually emerge as we organize and impose a pattern upon them. Teachers of writing were encouraged to nurture this process through such heuristic techniques as journal writing, meditation, and analogy.

Rohman describes prewriting as an introspective process of invention located within writers and meant to help writers express their experiences to themselves both before and while they communicate them to others. Such a view of invention presupposes a concept of the writer as a self-contained sphere of agency, "one," Rohman tells us, "who stands at the center of his own thoughts and feelings with the sense that they belong to him" (43). Contemporary practices of invention that encourage the use of prewriting heuristics such as freewriting, brainstorming, and clustering inherit the concept of the writer that informs them. Unlike the classical topoi, which were publicly available rhetorical strategies, these introspective heuristics assume that an individual possesses a priori topics "inherently there, waiting to be mined" (Ohmann 1976, 150). To "unlock discovery," for example, Rohman recommends the use of meditation as a heuristic. He advises students "to compose a *'place'* for your subject, one where you can live. Keep composing until you reach the point that your understanding of your 'subject' is experienced within, until, in other words, the 'event' of your subject happening to you becomes an experience happening within you" (46; my emphasis).

This advice marks a major turning point in invention theory, for it signals the rebirth of invention in composition. Rohman not only rejects current-traditional, product-based theories of writing, but he also rescues invention as the central canon of rhetoric. Yet his work maintains a privatized economy of invention as a "place" writers foster within themselves rather than as social "places" (topoi) to which writers turn in order to orient themselves within social methods of inquiry, as classical and tagmemic rhetoric had described. In a way that classical and tagmemic rhetoric could not, Rohman and Wlecke's work on prewriting gained credibility in part because it referenced and confirmed deeply held beliefs about authorship, beliefs that had been gaining momentum since the late eighteenth century as a result of copyright laws, Romantic theories of originality, literary assumptions about authorship, the influence of the printing press, and Enlightenment privatization of knowledge (LeFevre 1987; M. Rose 1993; Woodmansee and Jaszi 1994). Not only did Rohman and Wlecke's work draw on such beliefs; it also supported them by turning to contemporary work in creativity research, which was emerging as a subdiscipline of cognitive psychology at about the same time as the process movement was emerging.

## INVENTION AND/AS CREATIVITY

Rohman and Wlecke's research was heavily influenced by mid-twentieth century developmental psychology and creativity theory. Like their contemporary Janet Emig, they drew from

Brewster Ghiselin's collection of essays on creativity, *The Creative Process* (1952) and *The Paris Interviews: Writers at Work*, which began to be published in 1958; as well as Jerome Bruner's work on cognition and discovery published in the early 1960s (Crowley 1998, 195; Schreiner 1997, 88). In "The Uses of the Unconscious in Composing" (1964), for instance, Emig turns to the testimony and advice of artists in order to understand writing processes, claiming that contemporary textbooks rarely acknowledge "that writing involves commerce with the unconscious self and that because it does, it is often a sloppy and inefficient procedure for even the most disciplined and longwriting of professional authors" (7). Seven years later, in *The Composing Processes of Twelfth Graders*, Emig once again takes writing textbooks to task for encouraging students to use externally schematized sources such as topics for invention when they should focus more on a writer's personality and feelings, in short, a writer's psychology (1971, 16). It is not surprising, then, to find Emig beginning *The Composing Processes of Twelfth Graders* with a review of contemporary theories of literary creativity, including Joseph Wallas's four stages of creativity: preparation, incubation, illumination, and verification (17–19). Indeed, as Steven Schreiner has argued, Emig's work on composing, work that was to have such a profound influence on process theories and pedagogies, was predicated on a view of literary creation and authorship, one built on the assumption that writing reflects and serves the needs of its writer, who is also its primary agent (1997, 87, 100–102).

In identifying the writer as the point of departure for writing, Rohman and Wlecke's and Emig's work drew on the work of creativity researchers who were beginning to investigate how ideas, particularly novel ideas, are created in the mind. Such research was based on the assumption that the mind does not only combine what it takes in through sense impressions, but can also invent something valuable and new (Feldman et al. 1994, 1). Because creativity theorists were beginning to focus on the cognitive processes involved in creative production, and because the process movement in composition developed in part out of such research, we can learn a great deal about process-based theories of invention by turning to work in creativity theory, so I will briefly turn to it now. As I will argue, however, while such work helped describe the complex cognitive processes involved when writers invent, and encouraged writing teachers to treat student writers as agents of their own writing and to respect their writing choices in ways that greatly enhanced the teaching of writing, it nonetheless presented a partial view of this process by focusing on the writer as self-contained agent of invention rather than on the larger sphere of agency in which the writer as agent participates.

In *Changing the World: A Framework for the Study of Creativity*, Feldman, Csikszentmihalyi, and Gardner describe how, since the 1950s, modern creativity research, as a branch of cognitive science, has attempted to locate and describe the various cognitive traits creative individuals might possess (1994, 4), hence books such as Ghiselin's *The Creative Process* and *The Paris Interviews* which encourage creative individuals to describe such activities as their work habits, personality traits, and psychological states while composing.[6] Once observed, these traits could then be presumably taught to others. (Cognitive research into student writers' composing strategies is very much predicated on this mode of inquiry.) By the 1970s, Feldman et al. explain, creativity research became more specialized, focusing not on general cognitive traits but rather on the nature and development of creative thinking in specific fields or disciplines (12–15). And yet, the focus of research, while more domain specific, continued to be on the cognitive processes of the individual involved in creative thinking. For example, in *The Emerging Goddess* (1979), Albert Rothenberg locates creativity in a "form of cognition" he calls "janusian" thinking, a way of conceiving "opposing or antithetical ideas, images, or concepts . . . as existing side by side and operating simultaneously" (138, 139–40). In a suggestive statement, one which in many ways reflects the goals of the process movement, Rothenberg argues that his primary concern "is not

with whether the final [creative] product does or does not conform to objectively verifiable reality, intrinsic reality, or to any
other metaphysical criteria for truth, *but with the thought processes
responsible for the creation of that product"* (139; my emphasis).

Silvano Arieti's influential book, *Creativity: The Magic Synthesis*
(1976), also focuses on the thought processes involved in
creativity. Even though at the end of the book Arieti does admit
the need for what he calls a "creativogenic society," one which
provides the appropriate conditions for creative persons to
achieve their potential (312–25), his focus is ultimately on the
cognitive and precognitive stages of creative development as
they are seemingly abstracted from the forms of social organization that organize and generate cognition. For example, he
begins by taking recent creativity theories to task for neglecting
the unconscious thought processes that account for the "birth"
of ideas (20) and then calls for a more thorough use of what he
calls a "deep psychology" in creativity study (34).

This deep psychology traces the creative process back to
what Arieti calls its conceptual, primitive, and amorphous
stages, each respective stage reaching further back into the
private recesses of the mind. Arieti describes the origins of the
creative process as based in an individual's "amorphous cognition," which is not expressed in images, words, or even
thoughts, but instead as a form of preconscious cognition he
calls an "endocept." The endocept alone does not mean anything, not even to the individual in whom it occurs. Within the
individual, it just feels like an inspiration that is incubating. In
order for the endocept to become manifested in any way, it
must first be transformed into a concept that is meaningful to
its host, the individual, and then to others, the culture. This
occurs through the primary and secondary processes. Primary
processes are a form of "primitive cognition" in which what is
formless first enters the world of conscious signification, of
words and ideas. It is at this point that the endocept becomes
recognizable to its host and only to its host, since primitive cognition, while conscious, is very illogical. For example, primitive

cognition will identify and group objects according to whim, perception, or feeling, not according to any kind of culturally accepted systemic logic, classes, species, or categories. It is imagination running freely, moving unpredictably through metaphor and simile without being subjected to critical or evaluative judgments.

As Arieti warns, however, primitive cognition cannot be allowed to dominate the creative process. In fact, the very reason that lunatics or schizophrenics are generally not considered creative is because they do not progress from the primary to the secondary processes, and so have no means of socially forming or conceptualizing their imaginations. During the secondary processes, then, conceptual cognition dominates. As Arieti explains, conceptual cognition evaluates primitive cognition; it either affirms or denies the formulations of the primary processes. At this conceptual stage, the individual begins to consider how best to represent his or her primitive cognition to others, how, that is, to make it public through the use of already existing formal and rhetorical conventions such as appropriate syntactic and semantic rules, literary techniques, and genres.

According to Arieti, social conventions factor late in the cognitive processes. They allow creative individuals to synthesize and develop what they have already nurtured privately through endoceptual and primary cognitive processes. Still, this view ignores the extent to which cognition evolves not from the private to the social but is rather formed throughout life in organized linguistic interactions. Vygotsky (1986) offers a way to understand cognition in relation to, rather than as a precondition of, social action. Bazerman, for example, describes how, "from a Vygotskian perspective, the mediating communicative patterns [of various fields and activities] are tools both for action and cognition, or cognition in relation to action" (1997a, 305). As we learn patterns of action and interaction, we also acquire and practice related patterns of cognition that organize and generate these actions and interactions. Drawing on work in distributed cognition and activity theory, Freedman and

Smart describe how, "within specific activities, thinking, knowing, and learning are distributed among co-participants, as well as mediated through the cultural artifacts in place—artifacts that include semiotic, technological, and organizational structures" (1997, 240). Without denying that preconscious and libidinal structures exert a force of their own on individuals' cognitive development and attachments, we can also recognize that these structures are elicited by and operate in inescapable relation to ideological structures (Alcorn 2002, 25). Consciousness is an ongoing, dynamic social and discursive accomplishment.

In George Lakoff and Mark Johnson's *Metaphors We Live By* (1980) we see a way in which Arieti's cognitive processes might be recast in more thoroughly dynamic and social ways. Investigating how individuals learn and use metaphors, Lakoff and Johnson argue that, far from being hardwired into and stemming from our preconscious cognition, metaphors are actually social concepts we learn as part of our social and linguistic development. As already existing social conventions, metaphors structure the ways individuals conceptualize reality. For example, Lakoff and Johnson describe how a conceptual metaphor that we in contemporary Western culture live by, "argument is war," structures the way we experience and enact arguments. The resulting metaphors we create to describe how we argue—in fact, the way we actually argue—do not stem from some endoceptual, precoginitive process but from this larger conceptual metaphor we have available to us, so that, for instance, we might say, "He shot down all my arguments," or "If you use that strategy, he'll wipe you out" (4). The way that we re-*cognize* argument and describe it metaphorically is thus coordinated by our overarching cultural metaphors. Likewise, the conceptual metaphor "time is money," so prevalent a part of how we culturally talk and write about time, structures the various metaphorical ways we are able to conceptualize and experience time, even at the level of "primitive" cognition, since such a metaphor seeps into our most private, most intuitive understanding of what time is.

Process-based views of invention, informed by work in creativity theory such as Arieti's and by Jerome Bruner's work on cognition and discovery, largely continue to imagine the inventing writer as a cognitive free agent. While overlooking the systems of linguistic and social interaction that necessarily inform even early-stage cognitive processes, such a view of the writer has nonetheless helped writing teachers productively acknowledge and encourage the writer's agency. It has helped make the writer a more active and conscious participant in the writing process, one who makes decisions, shapes meaning and reformulates it while writing, and performs different activities at different stages of writing. But by focusing mainly on the writer as the agent of his or her cognitive processes, the writing process movement has provided only a partial view of invention. While the writer is certainly an agent of writing, to locate him or her as the prime agent is to ignore the agency that is already at work on the writer as he or she makes decisions, shapes meaning, and reformulates it. So while the writer may be the most visible agent of his or her writing processes, these processes take place within and against a larger sphere of agency that shapes them. To describe how these larger spheres of agency affect how and why writers invent, I will now turn briefly to work in composition studies that examines invention as a situated activity. Looking in particular at Karen Burke LeFevre's influential *Invention as a Social Act*, I will first describe how social views of invention locate writers within spheres of activity and then, turning to work in genre theory, I show how genres can give teachers, students, and researchers of writing specific access to these spheres of activities that build on and add to our understanding and teaching of invention.

## INVENTION AS A SOCIAL ACT

LeFevre's *Invention as a Social Act* was one of several important books published in the late 1980s and early 1990s to challenge the dominant assumption "that invention is the private, asocial act of a writer for the purpose of producing a text" (LeFevre 1987,

13). For example, Brodkey (1987) challenged the modernist view of the writer in composition; S. Miller (1989, 1991) identified the writer as a textual subject; Cooper (1989) described an ecological view of writing; Ede and Lunsford (1990) demonstrated how writers are never alone when they write; Crowley (1990) traced the privatization of invention in current-traditional rhetoric; and Faigley (1992) showed how postmodernist theories could inform notions of subjectivity in composition. More recently, Howard (1999) has examined how dominant notions of authorship continue to inform attitudes about plagiarism, and Halasek (1999) provides ways of thinking about writing from a dialogic perspective. This genealogy of work has helped identify and describe the systems of language, culture, and interpersonal and intertextual relations in which writers and writing take place, a larger system of agency in which the writer as agent participates.

Drawing on the work of Richard Young and Janice Lauer, for example, LeFevre argues that invention is thoroughly a social act, "first, an act that is generally initiated by an inventor (or rhetor) and brought to completion by an audience; and second, an act that involves symbolic activities such as speaking or writing and often extends over time through a series of social transactions and texts" (LeFevre 1987, 38). As LeFevre explains, this definition of invention is predicated on the following assumptions: that the inventing "self" is both socially influenced and socially constituted; that the language or other symbol systems individuals use to invent are communal, "socially created and shared by members of a discourse community"; that invention is more a continuative than an originative activity, built on already existing foundations of knowledge; that invention involves an interaction with others, whether through internal dialogue with real or imagined others, or through the actual participation of others such as collaborators, editors, critics, mentors, and patrons; and, finally, that invention is shaped and enabled by social collectives (institutions, bureaucracies, governments, paradigms, etc.) which structure the ideological boundaries not only of what inventing individuals assume to be knowable, doable, and possible, but also of how an invention comes to be received and evaluated by others (33–35).

According to LeFevre, invention includes not only how we discover and develop ideas, but also how we inquire into them in the first place, because invention involves the use of symbolic systems such as language. Following Ernst Cassirer, LeFevre argues that language does not mirror or copy an external reality; it helps constitute that reality (111). We come to know and understand the world around us by way of the language we have available to us, since language is a symbolic system that mediates between us and a reality out there. Invention, therefore, is not only social because it almost always involves more than one person, real or imagined; it is also social because it involves the use of language, which immediately connects even the most solitary inventor with others in a symbolic social collective. Even one's most private inquiry is ultimately social because it involves the use of language.

LeFevre's *Invention as a Social Act*, along with the work that it followed and the work that continues to follow it, helps teachers and researchers of writing recognize that there is more at work on invention than just the writer. There is a writer's social context, made up not only of others who help and hinder invention, but also of social collectives, "supra-individual entit[ies] whose rules and conventions may enable or inhibit the invention of certain ideas" (LeFevre, 80). These collectives, LeFevre explains, powerfully "serve to transmit expectations and prohibitions, encouraging or discouraging certain ideas, areas of investigation, methods of inquiry, types of evidence, and rhetorical forms" (34–35). When Frank D'Angelo, therefore, advises students to invent by reaching "into the recesses of your mind [and spinning] out of yourself a thread of thought that will develop into an orderly web" (1980, 34), he is overlooking the ideological and discursive formations that are already institutionally in place before the student has begun to write and that organize the student's cognition in textured ways. These formations include such genres as freewriting and clustering. In fact, D'Angelo's own metaphor breaks down when we realize that a web can never be a freestanding structure. Rather, it takes its shape in relation to its surroundings, so that whatever web a student spins (through his or her own agency) must take shape within an already existing social web (which gives shape to and motivates his or her agency). These social webs, informed by and articulated in language, comprise the social collectives within which individuals function. Their presence complicates our partial understandings of the writer as the primary agent of his or her desires by reminding us that desires are informed textually, ideologically, and materially. The work of LeFevre, S. Miller, Ede and Lunsford, Cooper, Howard, and others in composition studies has contributed mightily to our understanding of how writers participate within social, interpersonal, and textual formations.[7]

At the end of *Invention as a Social Act*, LeFevre calls for continued inquiry into "the *ecology of invention*—the ways ideas arise and are nurtured or hindered by interaction with social context and culture" (126; my emphasis). In the years since, scholars have taken up this call by examining the interpersonal, textual, material, and ideological nature of this ecology. In the remainder of this book, I build on and add to their work by turning to genre theory, which both recognizes and gives teachers, students, and researchers specific access to the dynamic relations and interplay of agency at work within textured spheres of activity. As I described them in chapter 2, genres are sites of action which locate writers within specific relations, practices, commitments, and subjectivities. Within such discursive ecologies, writers not only acquire and articulate specific desires, but they also participate in, resist, and enact the relations and activities bound up in and deployed through these desires. To identify genres as sites of action is also to identify them as sites of invention. As I hope the following example will begin to demonstrate, treating genres as such sites allows us to interrogate analytically how writers position themselves, consciously and unconsciously, within desires to act as well as how they articulate and fulfill these desires as bounded, recognizable, meaningful, and consequential actions. In giving teachers, students, and

researchers access to the ecology of invention, genres can provide a richer account of agency as well as a more useful means
for describing and teaching invention in composition.

## GENRE AS SITE OF INVENTION: THE EXAMPLE OF D. H. LAWRENCE

As I will discuss in more detail in the next chapter, genres are
indeed ecological. As rhetorical ecosystems, genres help
communicants recognize, act within, and reproduce recurring
situations. They rhetorically delimit the ways we conceptualize
our environments by "identifying a repertoire of possible actions"
as well as the possible intentions and identities we may assume
within those environments (Bazerman 1994a, 82). As such, it is
perhaps more accurate to say that invention does not so much
begin in the writer or even in some abstract social collective as it
begins when a writer locates himself or herself within the discursive and ideological formation of a genre and its system of related
genres. This is the case even when we are dealing with a literary
"author" who is ostensibly writing about "personal" experiences.
As the following example of D. H. Lawrence suggests, even those
writers whom we popularly designate as geniuses, whose work
seemingly emerges from some inspired and mysterious depth,
are actually constituted by the genres in which they write. The
literary genre Lawrence uses to explore and communicate his
"private" experiences in part shapes and enables how he invents
these experiences, so that the genre he turns to in order to
invent ends up simultaneously inventing him.

It is well known that Lawrence's *Sons and Lovers* is an autobiographical novel, a *Künstlerroman*. It is perhaps less known that
Lawrence also wrote a number of autobiographical poems at
the same time as he was writing *Sons and Lovers*. In both the
novel and the poems, Lawrence grapples with similar issues, in
particular his relationship to his mother, whom he names "Mrs.
Morel" in the novel (he names himself "Paul") and "She" in the
poems. Yet in each genre, a very different experience of the
relationship emerges. In the novel, for example, Lawrence's

father, Mr. Morel, is an imposing, interfering presence who in many ways represents the realism of the world that Paul is trying to avoid. Mr. Morel is an unavoidable function of the novel. It is in part his presence in the novel that precludes Lawrence from describing the mythic, idealized relationship with his mother that appears in the poems.

Part of the mythic, idealized relationship between Lawrence and his mother that is described in the poems can be ascribed to the absence of Lawrence's father from the poems. There is no counterpart to the Mr. Morel figure in the poems. Gone is the interfering, ugly, destructive force that Mr. Morel embodies in the eyes of Paul and his mother. In the poems, there is no drunk father, no coal dirt, no fighting, no financial troubles, no self-conscious Paul, no aggressive Mrs. Morel. Instead of Paul and Mrs. Morel there is "I" and "She." This rhetorical shift from proper nouns to personal pronouns transforms the specific to the universal. It takes a very real, context-specific relationship and makes it a timeless, almost mythic, relationship. "She" is no longer bound by name to a physical, identifiable being; no longer particularized by dialogue and title as wife to Mr. Morel, mother to Paul, William, Annie, and Arthur; no longer specified by her place in Bestwood, Nottingham, and so on. "She" becomes the essence of mother, lover, virginity, beauty, inspiration, as in the poem "The Bride," in which even on her deathbed, she is a beautiful bride:

> She looks like a young maiden, since her brow
> Is smooth and fair;
> Her cheeks are very smooth, her eyes are closed,
> She sleeps a rare,
> Still, winsome sleep so still, and so composed.
>
> Nay, but she sleeps like a bride, and dreams her dreams
> Of perfect things.
> She lies at last, the darling, in the shape of her dream,
> And her dead mouth sings
> By its shape, like thrushes in clear evenings. (1977, 464–65)

The poem provides a useful and telling contrast to the way Lawrence describes Mrs. Morel's death in the novel, which seems to resist such idealizations. Here is Mrs. Morel on her deathbed in *Sons and Lovers*:

> [Paul] heard a cart clanking down the street. Yes, it was seven o'clock, and it was coming a little bit light. He heard some people calling. *The world was waking.* A grey, deathly dawn crept over the snow. Yes, he could see the houses. He put out the gas. It seemed very dark. The breathing came still, but he was almost used to it. (1977, 397; my emphasis)

What is striking about this scene is its materiality. Mrs. Morel's march towards death is not accompanied by her "dead mouth" singing "like thrushes in clear evenings" as it was in "The Bride." Her death is not singular as it is in the poem, but rather takes place while a cart clanks beneath her window and people are heard calling to each other. Through the narrator, Lawrence seems aware that, indeed, the world *was* waking, and, quite frankly, getting on with its business. In addition, the bride-like face of the dying mother in the poem is replaced in the novel with a very different face: "She lay with her cheek in her hand, her mouth fallen open, and the great, ghastly snores came and went" (398). What is it that accounts for this difference between thrushes singing and ghastly snores? It is at least plausible to say that the genre Lawrence chooses in part organizes and generates not only how he perceives significant events in his life, but also how he invents them.

Not dependent on the detail, dialogue, characters, and narrator in the same way as the novelist, the poet D. H. Lawrence can universalize his personal experience, transcending proper names, time, and place. This universalizing quality of poetry allows Lawrence to remember his mother not as a snoring, decrepit old woman, but as the great mother/lover—the eternal beauty and essence of woman. Poetry does this by not insisting on a strictly linear ordering of time. As such, Lawrence can reconstruct the image of his mother without sacrificing, as he would in the novel, the unity of the plot. Poetry allows for a greater degree of abstraction. It rhetorically allows Lawrence to abstract his mother from the conditions that define her in the novel, so that she becomes husbandless and virginal. Lawrence writes:

> Now come west, come home,
> Women I've loved for gentleness,
> For the virginal you.
> Find the way now that you never could find in life,
> So I told you to die. (476)

She dies, it seems, so she could be reinvented into Lawrence's poetry.

Ian Watt, however, argues that the early novel resists such idealizations because of its realist orientation (1983). As a genre, the novel emerged as a rejection of universals, driven by a desire to record a seemingly naturalistic account of the "real" behavior of "real" people. This desired fidelity to human experience forced a collapse between interiority and exteriority, between the external material world and the internal psychological worlds of the people who inhabit it. Such a collapse implied that the characters within novels are bound to a particular time and place. Not only, for example, are individuals defined by time, especially past time, but they are also defined by their environment. In short, the nineteenth century novel is realistic because it embodies a circumstantial view of life, situating individuals both temporally and physically.

It is in its rejection of neoclassical universals and absolutes and its privileging of individual experience and perception that the nineteenth century novel resists idealizations. This is the genred orientation and commitment that Lawrence positions himself within. Any desire on the part of Lawrence to idealize his mother in *Sons and Lovers* is repressed by the novel's generic orientations and commitments, of which Mr. Morel is a part. Lawrence, for example, cannot ignore the fact that Mrs. Morel has a husband, that this husband works in the mines, drinks, and, in general, does not live up to her expectations. As one more personality in a cast of characters, all influenced by their time and place, Mrs. Morel cannot be abstracted from her conditions. If Lawrence decontextualizes her, she will lose her identity in the world of the novel. Because the novel as a genre requires a certain fidelity to the human experience in all its complexity, because, that is, the "realistic" novel's generic conventions demand that characters be situated, named beings who engage in specific dialogue, Lawrence, if he is to successfully write within this genre, must de-center, or, better yet, demythologize his perception of his mother. That is, he must invent her differently.

There is something to be learned about invention from this example, in particular, something about why and how writers acquire and articulate desires and intentions as they participate in genred sites of action, whether in literary representations or, as we will see in the next chapter, in actual social practices and relations. Positing genre in addition to the writer as the locus of invention suggests that invention is not only a process of intro-spection but also a process of socialization, a process of position-ing oneself within and managing one's way through a set of relations, commitments, practices, and subjectivities. In this case, the genres within which Lawrence chooses to write (and this choice is not as free as it seems, as we will see in the next chapter) become very much akin to situated topoi or common-places—socio-rhetorical sites and strategies of action—within which he locates and invents his "autobiography."[8] Each genre, then, represents a different topic or commonplace, a situated and typified way of rhetorically organizing, conceptualizing, relating to, and acting in our real or imagined environments. When Lawrence begins to think about writing his autobiography in a certain genre, he enters into that genre's discursive and ide-ological space, including what Bazerman calls its "repertoire of possible actions" (1994a, 82), and so is in part habituated to experience and narrate his life story in ways made possible by the genre's rhetorical conventions. In such a way is a writer a double agent, an agent of his or her actions as well as an agent on behalf of already existing social actions. By extending the sphere of agency in this way, we acknowledge that the writer participates in this agency, but is not its sole agent.

Obviously, there is much that could account for why Lawrence's intentions differ in the novel and the poems, including his working through of libidinal desires. However, I just do not think we can understand these intentions and desires independently of the genred discursive and ideological formations within which they are generated and operate. The genres Lawrence uses to articulate his experiences also locate him in positions of articulation. As the sites or topoi within which he invents, the genres both habituate Lawrence within a social motive and provide him with the rhetorical conventions for enacting that motive as invention. We need to pay more specific attention to the situated discursive conditions within and against which communication and communicators take place and are made possible—the conditions that prompt us to invent. Genres provide access to and help us to understand and describe these conditions, since genres do not just ideologically structure the way individuals conceptualize situations; they also provide individuals with the discursive means for acting within situations, so that genres maintain the social motives which individuals interpret and enact as intentions. In the next two chapters, I will describe how genres function as textured sites or topoi of invention that rhetorically maintain the social motives that shape and enable writers' intentions—maintain, that is, the desires they help writers fulfill. In the final chapter, I will argue for a pedagogy that makes visible and teaches students how to access these genred sites of action so that they can participate more critically and effectively as agents within this agency.

# 4

## CONSTRUCTING DESIRE
### *Genre and the Invention of Writing Subjects*

[P]erforming a genre concerns a joint agreement to
perform certain positionalities within an institutional
regime—to "be" or "become" certain kinds of subjects.
Crucial to "becoming" is the notion that the "self" that
writes or reads is assembled at the site of utterance, is
the point of convergence of a range of possible subject
positions brought into being at any particular historical
moment for the achievement of a social action.

GILLIAN FULLER and ALISON LEE,
"Assembling a Generic Subject"

A boundary is not that at which something stops but . . .
the boundary is that from which something begins its
presencing.

MARTIN HEIDEGGER, "Building, Dwelling, Thinking"

We cannot understand genres as sites of action without also
understanding them as sites of subject formation, sites, that is,
which produce subjects who desire to act in certain ideological
and discursive ways. Genres are defined as much by the actions
they help individuals perform as by the desires and subjectivities
they help organize, which generate such performances. For
example, the genres D. H. Lawrence writes in not only help him
organize and articulate different desires, especially in relation to
his mother; they also, as the Latin root of the word *genre* suggests,
help generate these different desires to enact that relationship.
In this way, genres are sites of action *as well as* sites of invention,
topoi in which invention takes place.

To offer that genres maintain and elicit the desires that they
help writers to fulfill, however, is not to suggest that writers are
simply the effects of genres. As Fuller and Lee point out, the

subject produced at the generic site of utterance is a "convergence of a range of subject positions" (2002, 215), each presumably with its own ideological and libidinal attachments and defenses. Although part of the work that genres perform is to assemble and recruit a particular subject position for the achievement of a particular social action, this assemblage does not and cannot entirely evict the multiple, sometimes competing, commitments that converge at this site of articulation. Certainly, some genres enforce their subjects more powerfully than others, but this subject formation is nonetheless a negotiated stance. As Robert Brooke and Dale Jacobs observe, "we're endlessly in negotiation with the internal structures of the ideas we're building and the external structures that come from what we know of [a particular] genre. In the process of this negotiation, our ideas are transforming themselves. So are the ways we think of ourselves as writers, the roles we use to describe ourselves" (1997, 216). This negotiation, which also includes the relationship between a writer's material, local conditions, and the genre's ideological and discursive demands, accounts in part both for how and why writers resist and transform genres and for textual variations within genres, as I will discuss later in the chapter. After all, no two texts within a genre are exactly alike. Each textual instantiation of a genre is a result of a unique negotiation between the agency of a writer and the agency of a genre's conditions of production. Because of this ongoing negotiation, generic conventions always exert influence over but do not completely determine how writers think and act because these conventions rhetorically maintain larger social motives (predispositions or desires to act) which writers acquire, negotiate, and articulate when they write. It is within the discursive and ideological space of genre—which I will later describe as the intersection between a writer's intentions and the genre's social motives—where agency resides. In this chapter, I examine this intersection in order to demonstrate how agency involves both the performance of an action as well as the construction of the desires that elicit such performance—in short, the processes by which writers are articulated by the very genres they use to articulate themselves, their commitments, relations, and social practices. Looking at several examples, I analyze how genres situate writers within such positions of articulation.[1]

### GENRES AS RHETORICAL ECOSYSTEMS

Human beings are rhetorical beings. We are not only different from other animals because of our capacity to use language as symbolic action or because we can use language to express ourselves in rhetorical ways; more significantly, we use language to construct rhetorical environments in which we exist, interact with one another, and enact social practices. We are constantly in the process of shaping our environments as we communicate within them, speaking and writing our realities and ourselves. Within these rhetorical constructs, we assume different subjectivities and relations, and we perform different activities as we negotiate our way from one environment to the next, often balancing multiple, even contradictory, subjectivities and activities at the same time. While on a visit to Florida a couple of years ago, I was struck by the extent to which this is the case. Seemingly everywhere, the geography of Florida is rhetorically demarcated by such slogans as "the *real* Florida" or billboards that promise real estate that allows one to "experience the *wild* in your backyard." These slogans and billboards ironically stand interspersed between billboards advertising the staged realities of Disney's Epcot Center and Universal Studios. Marking Florida's highways, these signs appear to be engaged in a rhetorical argument with one another: the "real" Florida versus the "tourist" Florida. But this binary does not hold. The "real" Florida is as much a rhetorical formation as is the "tourist" Florida. That is, Epcot is as complex and dynamic a discursive and ideological site as any wilderness-designated area; one is no less "artificial" than the other. Both are rhetorical demarcations—ways we organize, conceptualize, and participate within these formations—and both are at work in constructing the narrative of what we mean when we say what Florida "is."[2]

Anthony Petruzzi notes that "human beings dwell rhetorically through rhetoric's most primordial function: the 'making-known' of being which discloses the modes of human existence through articulated self-understanding" (1998, 310). Rhetorical practices not only help individuals communicate their realities to one another; they also help organize these realities. The Greek Sophists understood the contingent and rhetorical nature of human reality. Like the so-called "new rhetoricians" (Richards, Burke, Perelman) who followed them in our own century, the Sophists recognized that rhetoric is epistemological, involved not just in how we order particular arguments, but more significantly in how we order and come to know reality, which itself becomes a cultural argument or mythos writ large. The Sophists referred to this rhetorical construction of reality as *nomos*, what Susan Jarratt defines as "rhetorical construct" or "habitation" (1991, 42). Within this rhetorical habitation, human customs of social and political behavior are historically and provisionally situated and reproduced through cultural narratives, which, according to Kenneth Burke, shape the symbolic conditions in which we identify and relate to one another (1969b). These habitations, these nomoi, do not exist only on the symbolic level, however. As Jarratt explains, they are also realized syntactically and rhetorically so that, as the Sophists understood, rhetorical habits sustain the very habitats within which "reality" and "truth" get enacted. As the Sophists also understood and used to their advantage, a disruption of syntactic and rhetorical habits could also disrupt the social habitats upon which they are predicated. Our interactions with others and with our environments, therefore, are mediated not only by physical conditions but also by rhetorical conditions that, in part, are ideologically and discursively organized and generated through genres. Genres—what Catherine Schryer defines as "stabilized-for-now or stabilized-enough sites of social and ideological action" (1994, 108)—thus constitute typified rhetorical sites or habitations in which our social actions and commitments are made possible and meaningful as well as in which we are rhetorically socialized to perform (and potentially transform) these actions and commitments. As Carolyn Miller explains, "rhetoric provides powerful structurational resources for maintaining (or shoring up) social order, continuity and significance" (1994, 75). Genres rhetorically embody these structurational resources, helping "real people in spatio-temporal communities do their work and carry out their purposes" as well as helping "virtual communities, the relationships we carry around in our heads, to reproduce and reconstruct themselves, to continue their stories" (Miller 1994, 75). In this ecological scenario, genres coordinate a symbiotic relationship between rhetorical habits and social habitats.

Within material constraints, then, our social relations, subjectivities, commitments, and actions are rhetorically mediated by genres, which organize the rhetorical conditions within which we enact and reproduce our social relations, subjectivities, commitments, and actions. In this way, genres are not merely passive backdrops for our actions or simply familiar tools we use to convey or categorize information; rather, genres function more like rhetorical ecosystems, dynamic sites in which communicants rhetorically reproduce the very conditions within which they act. Within genres, therefore, our typified rhetorical practices support the very recurring conditions that subsequently make these rhetorical practices necessary and meaningful. This is why genres, far from being innocent or arbitrary conventions, are at work in rhetorically shaping and enabling not only social practices and subjectivities, but also the desires that elicit such practices and subjectivities.

We notice the extent to which genres function as rhetorical ecosystems (rhetorical habits and social habitats) if we look at the example of the physician's office. A physician's office is both a material and a discursive site in which doctor and patient interact. The genres used within this site coordinate this interaction. Prior to any interaction between doctor and patient, for example, the patient has to complete what is generally known as the Patient Medical History Form.[3] Patients recognize this genre, which they encounter on their initial visit to a physician's office, as one that solicits critical information regarding a patient's physical statistics (sex, age, height, weight, and so on) as well as medical history, including prior and recurring physical conditions, past treatments, and, of course, a description of current physical symptoms. This is followed by insurance carrier information and then a consent-to-treat statement and a legal release statement, which the patient signs. The genre is at once a patient record and a legal document, helping the doctor treat the patient and presumably protecting the doctor from potential lawsuits. But these are not the genre's only functions. The Patient Medical History Form (PMHF) also helps organize and generate the social and rhetorical environment within which the patient and doctor use language to interact and produce meaningful, situated action. For instance, the genre supports and enacts a separation between the mind and the body in treating disease, constructing the patient as an embodied object. It is mainly rhetorically concerned with a patient's physical symptoms, suggesting that we can treat the body separately from the mind—that is, we can isolate physical symptoms and treat them with little to no reference to the patient's state of mind and the effect that state of mind might have on these symptoms. In so doing, the PMHF reflects Western notions of medicine, notions that are rhetorically naturalized and reproduced by the genre and that in turn are materially embodied in the way the doctor recognizes, interacts with, and treats the patient as a synecdoche of his or her physical symptoms. (For example, it is not uncommon for doctors and nurses to say, "I treated a knee injury today" or "The ear infection is in room three.") The PMHF, then, locates the individual who completes it in the position of "patient" (an embodied self) prior to his or her meeting with the doctor at the same time as it works on the doctor who reads it, preparing him or her to meet the individual as an embodied "patient." So powerful is the socializing power of this genre in subject formation that individuals more often than not become willing agents of the desires embedded within it. As Tran explains: "Also on the [PMHF], there is a part that says 'other comments' which a patient *will understand* as asking whether or not he or she has any other physical problems, not mental ones" (1997, 2; my emphasis). Even when a patient ostensibly has a choice, the genre and the ideology it reflects and naturalizes are already at work constituting the patient's subjectivity in preparation for meeting the doctor. Thus, the genre compels individuals to assume certain situational positions, positions established by our culture and rhetorically articulated and reproduced by the genre.

The PMHF thus becomes a site for the material exchange of language within which the doctor and patient enact specific practices, positions, and relations. As a genre, it is both a habit and a habitat—the conceptual habitat within which individuals perceive and experience a particular environment as well as the rhetorical habit by and through which they function within that environment. But the PMHF does not function in an ecological vacuum. It is one of a number of genres (genres such as prescription notes, letters to insurance companies, referral letters, various medical records, etc.) that function in relation to one another and that together enable their users to maintain and participate in the situated activities that constitute the larger "ecosystem" we call the physician's office. Each of the genres in this constellation of interconnected, competing, and sometimes conflicting genres constitutes its own micro-environment—specific social situations, commitments, practices, and relations (relations between nurses and doctors, doctors and other doctors, doctors and pharmacists, doctors and insurance companies, and so on). Together, these genres—what Amy Devitt has called "genre sets" (1991)—interact to constitute the macro-environment we recognize as the physician's office. As a result, the physician's office becomes an intra- and intergeneric environment. Within this genre-constituted and genre-mediated macro-environment, communicants assume and enact various heterogeneous desires, language games, social practices, relations, and subjectivities—multiple ways of identifying themselves and relating to others in particular situations, much as we write ourselves into the position of patient in the PMHF and, in so doing, shape and enable not only our social practices and relations, but also "the ways we think of ourselves as writers, the roles we use to describe ourselves" (Brooke and Jacobs 1997, 216).

JoAnne Yates and Wanda Orlikowski, drawing on Bazerman (1994a), describe how "genre systems serve as organizing structures within a community, providing expectations for the purpose, content, form, participants, time, and place of coordinated social interaction" (2002, 104). By identifying a system of genres such as the one at work in the physician's office, researchers can examine how typified textual practices mediate complex forms of social organization. Carol Berkenkotter, for example, has recently demonstrated how psychotherapists and their clients are engaged in a network of related genres that synchronizes their activities and subjectivities. In the process of their interaction, for example, therapists and clients will engage in a number of genres, including the "client's narrative during the therapy session," the "therapist's notes" (which are taken during the session), and the "psychosocial assessment" (which the therapist writes after the session). Each of these genres, which Berkenkotter argues are coordinated in part by the meta-genre of the DSM IV (*Diagnostic and Statistical Manual of Mental Disorders*), maintains the rhetorical and ideological underpinnings for how therapist and client identify one another, interact, and perform their activities. As Berkenkotter explains:

> The psychotherapist's practice of making notes and reports that recontextualize the [client's] self-reports and interactions within psychiatric discourse begins the work of drawing the individual clients into the systems of reimbursement, health care, research, and medical reasoning. Perhaps even more importantly, psychotherapy notes and reports are the site at which we see the therapist constructing accounts that may influence how the clients themselves may begin to recontextualize their own perceptions of themselves. (2001, 341)

Taken together, these related genres coordinate the complex, multitextured social organization and activities of psychotherapy as well as "recontextualize" their users into different subjectivities within this organization.

Within systems of genre, some genres might perform regulative and managerial functions. For instance, Peter Medway

(2002) presents the difficult case of the architecture students' sketchbooks and wonders if these sketchbooks constitute a genre, especially since they do not share patterns of format, organization, or linguistic features—the traditional markers of genre. In fact, they do not even seem to produce an obvious typified social action. Part of Medway's conclusion, however, is that these sketchbooks do constitute a genre because of their affiliative function: by possessing them, students identify themselves as budding architects and practice the sensibilities that underwrite that subjectivity. While they may lack typified textual features, the sketchbooks can nonetheless be defined as a genre by the typified subjectivity—the architectural identity—they help their users perform (146). Even more interesting, however, is the function these genres might be serving in relation to the other architecture genres students are learning. Medway explains, for example, that these sketchbooks contain drawings, measurements, personal notes, formulas, maxims, notes, quotations, bibliographic information, pasted artwork, maps, building designs, drafts of arguments and texts, evaluations, and so on (131). Some of what the sketchbooks contain are examples of the other architecture genres students are expected to learn, which raises the question of whether this genre is not only a site of subject formation but also a site for regulating students' interaction within the generic system of relations of which it is a part. In this way, the sketchbooks enable students to acquire and practice the subjectivities and desires that facilitate their various genred performances within the architectural genre system.[4] In the remainder of the chapter, I analyze how writers position themselves within such genred ecologies and acquire, negotiate, and perform the desires and subjectivities that shape the choices they make when they write.

## MOTIVATING INTENTIONS: GENRE AND THE TRANSMISSION OF DESIRE

In "Building, Dwelling, Thinking," Martin Heidegger argues that we begin our "presencing"—our coming into being—within boundaries (1992). Similarly, Erving Goffman explains that "the individual . . . [is] a stance-taking entity, a something that takes up a position somewhere between identification with an organization and opposition to it. . . . It is thus *against something* that the self can emerge" (1961, 319–20; Goffman's emphasis). How does this identification and "becoming" happen within the ideological and discursive boundaries we call genres? How, that is, are "selves" always situated and hence always presencing into identity as they are recontextualized from one genred site of action to the next, even within a constellation of genres such as the physician's office or, as we will consider in the next chapter, a first-year writing classroom? Anthony Giddens's work in sociology can provide an answer.

The environment and its participants' activities and subjectivities are always in the process of reproducing one another within genre: the Patient Medical History Form, for example, rhetorically maintains the situational conditions within which doctor and patient enact their roles and activities, and their roles and activities in turn reproduce the very conditions that make the PMHF necessary and meaningful. Anthony Giddens, in *The Constitution of Society: Outline of the Theory of Structuration*, describes this ecological process as the "duality of structure" (1984). Giddens's theory of structuration is largely an attempt to reconcile what he perceives as inaccurately dichotomized views of human agency and social systems, what he calls "hermeneutic sociologies" ("the imperialism of the subject") versus "structuralist sociologies" ("the imperialism of the social object") (2). Both sociologies are inaccurate, Giddens argues, because they overlook the extent to which human actions both enact and reproduce social structures. In their social practices, human beings reproduce the very social structures that subsequently make their actions necessary, possible, recognizable, and meaningful, so that their practices reproduce and articulate the very structures that consequently call for these practices.[5] Genre is a site in which this dialectic of agency takes place.

For Giddens, structures, as I have been arguing about genres, do not merely function as backgrounds for social activities;

instead, they are "fundamental to the production and reproduction of social life" (36), including especially identity formation. Structures function on two simultaneous, homologous levels: the conceptual and the actual. On the one hand, structures are concepts, virtual rules and resources that exist ideologically and that dwell in memory traces regardless of whether we are conscious of them or not (25). They function on the level of ideology, as what Pierre Bourdieu calls "predispositions" (1990; 1998) that frame the ideological and epistemological boundaries of what we assume to be knowable, doable, or at least possible in any given situation. On the other hand, structures do not just have a conceptual existence, but are actualized as social practices that "comprise the situated activities of human agents, reproduced across space and time" (Giddens, 25). According to Giddens, social practices, manifested as certain technologies, conventions, rituals, institutions, tools, and so on, materialize structures. These structural practices are the social means (the tools, resources, conventions) by which we put ideology into practice, the means by which we enact ideology as social action. Thus, they allow human agents to enact and hence reproduce ideological structures—the two recursively interact to form a "duality of structure" on both an epistemological and ontological level. Structures, in short, are both the ideology and the enactment of the ideology. As Giddens explains, "the rules and resources drawn upon in the production and reproduction of social action are at the same time the means of system reproduction" (19). Referring back to our discussion in chapter 2 of Halliday's work (1978) on language as social semiotic, we can compare structures to what Halliday calls "semantic potential" and social practices to what Halliday calls "actualized potential" so that structures constitute the potential for action, and social practices, recursively working within structures, constitute the actualization of that potential. As such, structures both provide a defined, socially recognized, and ideological action-potential (what individuals can do in a given situation) as well as the means of instantiating that potential as actualized social practice in space and time (what individuals actually do in a given situation).

Insofar as structure represents the ideological potential for action, it is linked to "motive." According to Giddens, motive exists on the conceptual level of structure, meaning that it is already conceptually built into the structural framework of a situation. He explains, for instance, that "motivation refers to potential for action rather than to the mode in which action is chronically carried out by the agent. . . . For the most part motives supply the *overall plans or programmes* . . . within which a range of conduct is enacted" (6; my emphasis). Given this explanation, we can combine Halliday and Giddens to define structure as a motive-potential which frames the possible ways of acting and meaning in any given time and space. Operating on the conceptual level of structure, motive frames the ideological boundaries that socially define and sanction an appropriate "range of conduct" within a particular situation, thereby regulating the possible ways we can act in a specific situation. This notion of motive is related to what Carolyn Miller has defined as exigence. If exigence, as Miller argues, is "a form of social knowledge," a learned recognition of significance that informs how and why we respond to and in a situation, then, indeed, exigence constitutes "an objectified social need" (1984, 157) or motive-potential for action. In short, exigencies inform our desires to act in certain situations and under certain conditions. Often, social motives are so sedimented a part of our social knowledge, so ideologically naturalized, that we as social actors are unaware of their constitutive presence. Motive becomes such a part of what seems our "natural" or logical desire to act that we no longer consider the ideologies that compel our actions. We rarely pause to consider how or why we come to recognize a situation as requiring a certain action. We just act.

We function, then, within motive-potentials that constitute in part what Giddens calls structures. But, as we discussed earlier, structures are not just potentials and desires; they are also actualizations of potential and desire. In order for us to actualize the potential for action—in order, that is, for us to become agents of social motives—we must internalize and transform social motive into individual action, and this is where intention comes into play. Intention is where motive-potential becomes internalized by actors and then articulated as agency. Whereas motive is socially defined, intention is an individualized interpretation and instantiation of social motive. Intention is a form of social cognition—an embodiment of desire and the means by which individuals become social agents, interpreting and carrying out the social motives available to them. According to Giddens, intention can only exist *in relation to* motive, since "for an event to count as an example of agency, it is necessary at least that what the person does be intentional *under some description*, even if the agent is mistaken about that description" (8; my emphasis). Intention must have some socially defined motive in order to be recognized as a meaningful social action, something that gives it generalizable meaning and value within a particular environment. It must be intentional under some *described* social motive. Yet whereas motive is largely unconscious, intention is conscious, goal-driven, and spatially and temporally bound. Intention is, finally, the acquisition, negotiation, and articulation of motive as social practice, motive being the desire within and against which individuals enact their intentions *and* their agency—their coming into being, their presencings.

The "motive-intention" interaction described above is situated within and reproduces structure, which provides both the ideological conditions and the socio-rhetorical conventions agents need for enacting their social practices. These practices, in turn, reproduce the very structures they enact. This recursive process at work in what Giddens calls structures is similar to the one I have been describing as at work in genres. Genres are structures in that they maintain the ideological potential for action in the form of social motives and the typified rhetorical means of actualizing that potential in the form of social practices. Genres are ideological concepts and material articulations of these concepts at once, maintaining the desires they help individuals fulfill. This actualized activity (the patient completing the PMHF, for instance) reproduces the ideological conditions—how physicians conceptualize their practices and respond to their patients—that in turn result in the kind of patient-physician interaction that prompted the PMHF in the first place. Intention is where motive is enacted as socio-rhetorical action, and socio-rhetorical action is where motive is reproduced as ideology, so that the enactment of motive as intentional action reproduces the very motive that made it possible. Genre is central to this ecological process.

Returning to Heidegger (1992), then, we notice that genre is both the boundary and the presencing, both the ideological construction of a situation and its rhetorical enactment—in short, the boundary that makes presencing possible. To assume, therefore, that the writer is the locus of invention because he or she is the most immediate agent of his or her intentions is to overlook the larger spheres of agency, such as genres, which organize and generate writers' desires to act. We will now look at some examples of how writers act as they are acted upon by genres.

## GENRE AND THE INVENTION OF WRITING SUBJECTS

The power of genre resides, in part, in this sleight of hand, in which social obligations to act become internalized as seemingly self-generated desires to act in certain discursive ways. This does not mean, however, that writers' desires are completely determined, as evidenced by the fact that textual instantiations of a genre are rarely if ever exactly the same. Every time a writer writes within a genre, he or she in effect acquires, interprets, and to some extent transforms the desires that motivate it. As such, every articulation necessarily involves an interpretation, which means that different writers will interpret, to some extent, the same genre motive slightly differently, based on their social and psychological experiences, the demands of their immediate conditions, their social position and location within the larger sphere of culture, their metacognitive awareness of the genre, their knowledge of other genres, and so on. Genre motive alone thus does not "do" anything; it is a potential that requires individual interpretation and articulation in order for the motive to become actualized as social action. As a result, genres "are always sites of contention between stability and change. They are inherently dynamic, constantly (if gradually) changing over time in response to the sociocognitive needs of individual users" (Berkenkotter and Huckin 1993, 481). This is why no two texts within a genre are exactly alike and also why genres are not completely deterministic. Genres exist at the intersection between the writer as agent of his or her actions and the writer as agent on behalf of already existing social motives.

And so, although genres exert influence over situations and individuals' desires to act within them, there is still room for their users as agents to enact slightly different intentions or even to resist the ideological pull of genres in certain circumstances. Of course, such resistance—to be recognized and valued as resistance and not misinterpretation or, worse, ignorance—must be predicated on one's knowledge of a genre. For example, writers who successfully transgress certain genres often do so because they have established a certain degree of authority in the sphere in which the genres function coupled with a critical awareness of the genres' conventions, in particular what habits of mind are underwritten by these conventions and which of these conventions can be transformed to greatest effect. The intention and the ability to transgress genres is thus *still* connected to the knowledge of the social motives that these genres maintain and articulate. Certainly, some genres—Peter Medway calls them "baggy genres"—provide more room for transgression than others (1998). Generally, we think of literary genres as "baggy" in this sense, meaning they allow for more resistance and playfulness than most nonliterary genres. In fact, they elicit this playfulness as part of the very motive that writers must internalize in order to become considered "creative" writers. Conversely, patients completing the PMHF are less likely to have the same playful intentions, being motivated by different situational exigencies, so that if a patient were, say, to describe his or her symptoms using personification and an allegorically based dialogue between various body parts, he or she would either be denied treatment or, more likely, be asked to receive psychological treatment instead, a move, ironically, that then situates that individual in another genre system with its own set of relations, subjectivities, commitments, and practices, as Berkenkotter has described in her study of psychotherapy genres. In any case, in doing so the individual has probably succeeded in resisting the patient subject position that the PMHF compels—opting instead, ironically, for a different, perhaps more literary, genre identity—but in so doing, the individual has altered not only the situation into which he or she was attempting to enter, but also the potential relationship between himself or herself and the doctor as well as perhaps even the kind of treatment he or she might receive.[6] In short, the individual has most likely written himself or herself out of one site of discursive and ideological action and into another.

To be sure, then, there is room for resistance and transformation within genres, some genres more than others. And any account of invention, including this book's, must take this into account. The potential for resistance and transformation, however, does not preclude the fact that invention takes place within genres, within the social motives that are sustained rhetorically by generic conventions. As such, transgression, which itself depends on the conventions it seeks to resist, remains a function of genre. According to Brooke and Jacobs, "genre is a site of identity negotiation. . . . Our relationship to genre as writers, thus, follows the same logic as our relationship to social roles as individuals. In the same way we create a self by negotiating our stance toward the social roles we inhabit . . . so we create our self *as writer* by negotiating our stance toward the genres we use" (1997, 217; Brooke's and Jacob's emphasis). Regardless of how we may position ourselves within genre-mediated situations, then, the point remains that we write and speak ourselves in relation to the social and rhetorical conditions we call genres. As Bazerman explains, "through an understanding of the genres available to us at any time we can understand the roles and relations open to us" (1994a, 99). These roles and relations are articulated in various genres, some more powerfully than others, so that these already available subject positions will inform but never completely determine our more immediate circumstances as writers.

We find remarkable evidence of this phenomenon in Kathleen Jamieson's research on antecedent genres, which complicates Lloyd Bitzer's now classic notion of rhetorical situation by exploring the role that genres play in shaping rhetorical action. Bitzer regards rhetorical situation as "a natural context of persons, events, objects, relations, and an exigence which strongly invites utterance" (1968, 303). According to Bitzer, the context and exigence that form the basis of a rhetorical situation have an ontological status as "real, objective, historical events" existing independently of human definition (C. Miller 1984, 156). That is, the situation that calls for a rhetorical response exists prior to and independently of our rhetorical participation. Jamieson counters, however, that when individuals are faced with an unprecedented rhetorical situation, they often respond *"not merely from the situation* but also from antecedent rhetorical forms" or genres (1973, 163; Jamieson's emphasis). These carry with them the social knowledge individuals have of particular situations (what Giddens refers to as motive) as well as the rhetorical conventions for enacting that knowledge as social action (what Giddens calls intention). As antecedent forms, then, genres constitute the ways we perceive situations, including unprecedented situations, as well as the ways we define our positions within them—that is, they maintain the motives that make our intentions possible.

As an example, Jamieson cites George Washington's response to "the Constitutional enjoinder that the President from time to time report to Congress on the state of the union and recommend necessary and expedient legislation" (1975, 411). Faced with this unprecedented situation, the first president of the United States, who had earlier led a successful rebellion against the British monarchy, promptly responded by delivering a state of the union address "rooted in the monarch's speech from the throne" (411). That is, Washington adopted an already existing genre to respond to the demands of a new situation, a situation, ironically, that had emerged as a reaction against the situation appropriate for that antecedent genre. Even more remarkably, this presidential address, so similar to the "king's speech" in style, format, and substance, in turn prompted a response from Congress which, far from being critical of the president's speech, reflected the "echoing speech" that the House of Parliament traditionally delivers in response to the king's speech (411). As Jamieson explains, "the parliamentary antecedent had transfused the congressional reply with inappropriate characteristics," characteristics which not only masked an approval not felt by all members of Congress, but also, "because patterned on a genre designed to pay homage and secure privileges," carried "a subservient tone inappropriate to a coequal branch of a democratic government" (413).

What Congress was responding to in its reply to Washington's state of the union address was *not* so much the rhetorical situation as Bitzer describes it as it was the genre function as embodied by the "king's speech." Members of Congress assumed a subject position motivated by the king's speech and consequently enacted that role by responding in ways that were made possible by the "echoing speeches" of Parliament. One genre thus created the socio-rhetorical condition for the other in what Anne Freadman has called an "uptake," a concept adapted from speech act theory to refer to the inter- and intrageneric relationship between texts, in which one text—the king's speech—prompts an appropriate response or uptake from another—the echoing speech—in a particular context or ceremonial (1988, 95; see also 2002). "Patterning the first presidential inaugural on the sermonic lectures of theocratic leaders," Jamieson claims, "prompted an address consonant with situational demands" (1975, 414), demands motivated by the genres communicants had available to them. Antecedent genres thus play a role in constituting subsequent actions, even acts of resistance. Despite efforts to resist monarchical practices, Washington, perhaps unconsciously, assumed a monarchical position when he wrote his state of the union address as a king's speech, turning to an already textured position to respond to a more immediate and idiosyncratic circumstance. Aware of the powerful constraints antecedent genres impose, Jamieson asks: "How free is the rhetor's choice from among the available means of persuasion?" (1975, 414) She answers:

> To hold that "the rhetor is personally responsible for his rhetoric regardless of genres," is . . . to become mired in paradoxes. We would by that dictum have to interpret our founding fathers as deliberately choosing monarchical forms while disavowing monarchy . . . but those rhetors would be held "personally responsible" for rhetorical choices that in fact they did not freely make. (414–15)

It took until Woodrow Wilson's 1913 presidential address for the state of the union address to completely break from its generic antecedent—one hundred and twenty three years (Jamieson 415). Uptakes, Freadman reminds us, have memories—indeed, very long memories (2002).

Jamieson's research illuminates the role that genres play in constituting not only the ways we respond to and function within unprecedented situations, but also the subject positions we assume in relation to these situations. Genres have this generative power because they maintain the desires that elicit their use—socially sanctioned motives for "appropriately" recognizing and behaving within certain recurring situations—which become part of our intentions as social agents and which we then enact rhetorically as social practices. So even when unique circumstances such as the first state of the union address and the democratic ideals on which it is based call for new intentions—require the invention of something "new"—George Washington, as the writer of this address, performs a subjectivity that is informed in part by the desires embedded in the "king's speech." Washington's intention to invent, thus, does not simply stem from some deep-seated impulse located within him, as popular theories of invention would have us believe. The first state of the union address does not begin only with Washington, although he is certainly the most visible agent of that beginning. Rather, Washington invents by locating himself within the social motives embedded rhetorically in an already existing genre, which represents a larger sphere of agency within which his own agency takes place. Invention, in this case, is an act of turning outward, not just inward, a way of positioning oneself rhetorically and ideologically at the same time as it is a way of discovering and exploring ideas. When we consider the locus of invention, therefore, we need to look not only at the writer, but also at the genre within which the writer functions. We need to look, that is, at how the writer—whether it is George Washington or D. H. Lawrence—acts as he or she is acted upon. As Anthony Paré and Graham Smart conclude, after conducting research into the workplace genre activities of social workers and bank employees, genres conventionalize collective roles "despite the idiosyncrasies of the various individuals who fill the roles" (1994, 150). Such conclusions challenge us as scholars and teachers of writing to expand and complicate our notions of agency in ways that more fully account for how and why writers invent.

Because they are so entrenched in how we are socialized to respond to recurring situations, genre-constituted desires, subjectivities, and practices are difficult but not impossible to resist. Genres change, among many other reasons, because writers, over time, challenge the genre positions and relations available to them, especially when these positions and relations conflict with other subject positions and relations—gendered, racial, class-based, ethnic—that constitute writers' experiences, as in the case of Patricia Williams, whose *The Alchemy of Race and Rights* (1992) transgresses legal genres by introducing the element of autobiography. This autobiographical turn in legal studies seeks to undermine the ostensibly "objective" nature of legal discourses, in much the same way as ethnography seeks to expose the subjective nature of quantitative research (Helscher 1997, 32–33). But the fact remains that Williams is using autobiography, another genre, to subvert already existing legal genres, which means that she is turning to one subject position, this time an autobiographical one, in order to resist another subject position, that of an objective, rational lawyer. Autobiographically, Williams is positioned as a chronicler of events—one who has acquired what Brad Peters calls "an autobiographical grammar" that allows her to name the self, contextualize the self, and detect "thematic patterns in the development of the self" (1997, 204). These patterns form the autobiographical plot that organizes the life being narrated. As Eileen Schell notes, in the "autobiographical tradition, there is a double referent in the 'I' who writes—the 'I' who is constructed as the Subject in the current narration of events, and the 'I' who remembers the past events and reconstructs them" (1997, 172). Quoting Shari Benstock's work on autobiography and authority, Schell describes how "the 'gaps in the temporal and spatial dimensions of the text itself are often successfully hidden from the reader *and writer*, so that the fabric of the narrative appears seamless, spun of whole cloth.' . . . This 'seamless' autobiographical writing is magical, 'the self appears organic,' and the writer appears to have control over her subject matter" (1997, 172; my emphasis). To assume, then, that autobiography in some way enables writers to express a more authentic self, something more "personal" or "inherent" in order to resist the apparent objectivity of law, is to overlook the power of genre, any genre, to shape and enable writers' identities even as they transform the genre.[7]

Writers, of course, do not occupy only one genre position. They assume multiple positions and relations as they enact various social practices, both within genre systems and between genre systems. These subject positions and relations are always shifting, always multiple, as they are enacted by individuals within different genres. These positions also carry with them the ideological and libidinal desires that inform them, and which are manifest in terms of various attachments, values, repressions, and defenses. Within genre systems, as we saw in the case of the architecture students' sketchbooks, some genres function to organize and regulate these multiple subjectivities and desires, giving them a kind of coherence and logic. Janet Giltrow has recently described this unifying principle at work within a system of genres as "meta-genre" (2002). Metagenres are not genres per se, but more like "atmospheres surrounding genres" (Giltrow, 195) which provide the background knowledge and assumptions that tie the genres together and sanction their use, "patrolling or controlling individuals' participation in the collective" and "foreseeing or suspecting their involvements elsewhere" (203). On the one hand, a metagenre helps organize individuals' multiple subjectivities and desires within a genre system in such a way that it reduces the potential friction between these multiple subjectivities and desires. It works to repress conflict. On the other hand, individuals carry this meta-generic knowledge with them from one collective to the next, and it is when one metagenre conflicts with another that the possibility for resistance and transformation arises.

Although writers occupy various subject positions, they are not committed to these positions evenly. Because of training, experience, attachment, and/or proclivity, a writer may certainly feel more "at home" in one genre position than another. Such a default or alpha genre position travels with the writer as he or she negotiates various and contradictory genre positions and practices from situation to situation and from day to day. As Marshall Alcorn explains, "subjects contain a great deal of discourse, but some modes of discourse, because they are libidinally invested, repeatedly and predictably function to constitute the subject's sense of identity" (2002, 17). This alpha position and its discursive attachments could very well inform the different subject positions the writer assumes, affecting how the writer, in these different subject positions, interprets and performs different genred desires. Such attachments to certain subjectivities and desires, Alcorn reminds us, are very durable, and individuals will aggressively defend them, which explains both why certain genres persist even when they no longer serve their user's best interests (as we saw in the example of the state of the union address) and why writers will resist certain genres that conflict in some way with their commitments. The multiplicity of subject positions and desires within and between genre systems, thus, while it certainly makes transgression possible, does not mean that transgression is motivated by an extradiscursive, pre-rhetorical inherent intention. As Nikolas Rose proposes:

> Resistance—if by that one means opposition to a particular regime for the conduct of one's conduct—requires no theory of agency [as popularly conceived as self-willed]. It needs no account of the inherent forces within each human being that love liberty, seek to enhance their own powers or capacities, or strive for emancipation, that are prior to and in conflict with the demands of civilization and discipline. (1996, 35)

More accurately, resistance arises from the contradictions individuals experience in their multiple subject positions—in their "constant movement across different practices that subjec-tify them in different ways" (Rose, 35). What appears as an inte-rior desire to resist generic conventions and identities might actually be what Rose calls a "kind of infolding of exteriority" (36), an effort on the part of writers to work internally through the contradictory subject positions and relations they assume as they write various genres.

As Pierre Bourdieu explains it, resistance and change occur when there is a breakdown in logic between practice and ideol-ogy, that is, when individuals begin to experience a tension between the materiality of their practice and the "systems of structured, structuring dispositions" that Bourdieu calls "habi-tus" (1990, 52). The habitus endows practices with a "logic" or "common sense." But when the actual conditions of practice no longer support the "common sense" that underscores and moti-vates them, a breakdown in logic occurs that the habitus can no longer sustain. Such is the case with genres, which also predis-pose specific practices by endowing them with a certain com-mon sense. When a breakdown occurs between the writer as agent *of* his or her actions and the writer as agent *on behalf of* the genre, writers, as we saw in the case of Patricia Williams, can try to transform the genre to make it reflect more accurately the actual conditions of practice.[8]

Genres, then, shape and enable our positions as writers, even as they serve as the potential sites of resistance, because they maintain powerful desires which writers work within and against as they move from one situation to the next. This process of socialization and transformation takes place discursively, and is dramatized in the ways that individuals are taught and learn to write (see, for example, Bartholomae 1985; Bazerman 1994a; Berlin 1987; Bizzell 1992; Brodkey 1987; Cooper and Holzman 1989; Faigley 1992; Freedman 1993a; Lu 1991; Schryer 1994; Villanueva 1993). Anthony Paré, who for years has studied the role of writing in the socialization processes of social workers, describes how this process works. One genre social workers frequently write is the "assessment report," which contains a social worker's initial review of a client's condition and needs. In his research, Paré observes that the assessment report, like other social work genres, is loaded with such "self-effacing constructions as 'the undersigned believes' and 'the worker recommends,' as well as completely self-erasing phrases, such as 'it is believed,' 'the assessment is based on,' and 'recommendations include the following'" (1998, 1). These rhetorical self-erasures, meant to mimic the ostensible certainty of science and its positivistic observation of phenomena, is common in social work, "where allegiance to 'objectivity' is like a professional mantra" (2), socializing employees into the institutional life of social work. Interestingly, however, Paré finds no "official" documentation of this mantra: "Although I have not in 10 years of looking actually found a printed or explicitly stated regulation against the use of the first person pronoun, and despite the fact that students and workers are often not clear why they shouldn't use it or who told them not to, there is almost universal obedience to the rule in social work" (1–2). We can, following Giddens, speculate that such a rule exists on the ideological level of genre, where motive has a virtual existence as "objectified social need" and where individuals enact motives unconsciously, only aware of them as they are instantiated in textual and social practices. In any case, when social workers enact their institutionally motivated "professional, disembodied persona" (Paré, 4) in such genres as the assessment report, they are at once rhetorically instantiating as their intention that motive for objectivity and, in turn, recursively reproducing that motive as part of social work ideology. In short, they are writing themselves into the very conditions that they are reproducing in their writing.

Paré's research shows how writers acquire desires and subjectivities as they learn to write genres. For example, the following transcript from a discussion between a social work supervisor and a student named Michael reveals the early stages of this socialization. The student asks, "It has to be impersonalized as in 'the worker,' even if it's you, you have to say 'the worker'?" (2002, 67). The supervisor's answer is illuminating, and so I cite it in its entirety:

> That's right. So you wrote here, "I contacted." You want to see it's coming from the worker, not you as Michael, but you as the worker. So when I'm sometimes in Intake and [working] as the screener, I write in my Intake Notes "the screener inquired about." . . . So it becomes less personal. You begin to put yourself into the role of the worker, not "I, Michael." . . . [I]t's a headset; it's a beginning. And even in your evaluations . . . the same thing: as opposed to "I," it's "worker," and when we do a CTMSP for placement for long-term care, "the worker." So it positions us, I think. It's not me, it's my role; and I'm in the role of a professional doing this job. (Paré 2002, 67; my emphasis)

What does the supervisor mean by "it's a headset; it's a beginning"? A beginning of what? According to Heidegger, this beginning could refer to the moment of presencing that begins in relation to boundaries, the moment when the supervisor becomes "interpellated" or "hailed"—to borrow terms from Louis Althusser—by the genre into the subject position of social worker. As Althusser formulates it, ideology interpellates individuals as subjects, who actualize that potential both in the texts they produce and the identities they assume as social workers. This process of interpellation works consensually, Althusser insists, by making it appear as though we are *choosing* the subject position imposed on us, choosing, that is, our own subjectivity (1984). As the supervisor tells the student, "*You* begin to put *yourself* into the role of the worker." This interpellation is what the patient undergoes as he or she completes the Patient Medical History Form in the physician's office. It is the process of presencing into subjectivity that the supervisor alludes to—in this case, the process by which the student, Michael, becomes positioned by the assessment report into the role of professional "doing this job." Once again, writers begin to write by locating themselves within rhetorical ecosystems we call genres. It is within genres that writers invent themselves, their subjects, and their texts.

As a writer, Michael occupies multiple subject positions both within social work genre systems and within various other genre systems. He might be a patient, a social worker, a student (and as a student, a first-year writing student, a sociology student, a physics student, and so on), a defendant, a job candidate, and so on. Each of these positions is mediated by a variety of genres at work within the various situations and activities Michael encounters and performs everyday.[9] To say, then, that the assessment report is a self-effacing genre, as some might claim, may not be entirely accurate. It is not so much that the genre is self-effacing as it is self-constructing, although this constructed self may very well repress the other possible selves that could be performed in this genred site of action. The emerging professional persona that the assessment report helps make possible is no less a self than the self that emerges from writing more intimate, "personal" genres, such as the classroom "log" or "journal." Recall, for example, D. Gordon Rohman's suggestion (described in the previous chapter) that teachers should encourage student writers to keep journals as a way of discovering themselves (Rohman 1994, 44–45). Rohman's assumption is that the journal, as a genre, allows students to access and actualize their true selves, to establish, in the words of one of Rohman's students, "a discovery of myself" (45). In fact, however, Aviva Freedman and Peter

Medway argue that the classroom journal, promising to provide students with the opportunity to express and explore their thoughts in a manner unfettered by formal conventions and strict rules of argumentation, actually constitutes a new set of institutional conventions, conventions seemingly overlooked by Rohman and others who espouse an introspective theory of invention (Freedman and Medway 1994b). As Freedman and Medway explain, "although the writer's focus was now claimed to be solely on thinking about the topic, the rhetorical demands had not disappeared; they had simply taken a new form" (1994b, 17). The new rhetorical demands made by the journal required a "self" as constructed as the more restrictive social work self constructed by the assessment report. Although the generic criteria of the journal were not made explicit, research by Barnes, Barnes, and Clark revealed that

> clever students knew they were there and learned to manipulate textual features to create an impression of artless expression. The genres the successful students evolved were an effective response to the new rhetorical exigence, part of which was an expectation that texts be produced of a certain length, expressivity, unconventionality, and sparkiness and that they mix observations about the material with indications of personal enjoyment, frustration, or amusement. Many of the texts fulfilling these expectations were indeed refreshing and delightful; less apparent at the time was that they were refreshing and delightful works of literary artifice. (Freedman and Medway, 17–18)

The classroom journal, then, like the assessment report, locates the writer within a discursive and ideological formation, in which he or she acquires, negotiates, and articulates particular desires, subjectivities, and activities. Even a genre like freewriting, which gives the illusion of a free space from which writers can begin to write, situates writers, consciously or unconsciously, within positions of articulation. As such, rather than assuming the writer to be the primary locus of invention, we should think of the writer as always positioned by genre within situated desires in order to perform certain social practices in a certain rhetorical manner.

Rather than claiming that a certain genre "effaces" self, then, it is perhaps more accurate to say that a certain genre replaces or, better yet, adds to the range of possible selves that writers have available to them. This way, we avoid problematic claims such as the ones Lester Faigley and Randall Popken make about the way the résumé as a genre ironically asks job candidates to construct a self while formally and rhetorically denying that self (Faigley 1992, 140-42; Popken 1999, 92–93). Faigley, for instance, describes how "agents are consistently deleted in résumé descriptions" in such subjectless sentences as "Maintained power control packages" and "Performed and supervised technical training of personnel" (141). In addition, social actions become represented as abstract nouns such as "sales effectiveness" and "personal relationships," all together leading to the representation of the agent in an abstract nominal style which renders him or her absent (141). Certainly, these résumé conventions, along with others, such as the generic categories ("career objectives," "work experience," "education") in which candidates must represent themselves; the spatial limitations (one or, at most, two pages); and the "topical prohibitions" (generally, no discussion of home life, nonwork interests, and so on) all impose severe limitations on how a writer represents himself or herself in this genre (Popken 1999, 92–93). Doubtless, these generic conventions elicit the writer of the résumé into the subject position of "job candidate," a commodified subject trying to sell himself or herself by embodying his or her skills, work experiences, and education (Faigley, 142). But to make this claim is not then to conclude that the résumé effaces its writer's subjectivity (142) or, for that matter, that "the résumé has few properties that permit writers to reveal 'presence' . . . a sense of *an individual human being who produced the document*" (Popken, 93; Popken's emphasis). If anything, actually, the résumé invokes presence, a particular résumé identity that is as "real" as any other genre identity that writers have available to them. To a great extent, writers will be more attached to one

genre identity than to others, perhaps because it is a subject position they most frequently occupy and so seems more "natural," or
because they feel emotional attachment to it, or because it is one
in which they are most successful, or because it is a position that
aligns them with institutions of power. This default or alpha identity will push up against the genres a writer encounters, from the
most to the least "personal," but nonetheless, these genres maintain the situational conditions within and against which individuals invent and define themselves as participants.

## GREETING CARDS AND THE ARTICULATION OF DESIRE

I will conclude this chapter by briefly analyzing how even
"humble genres" (Bazerman 1997a, 298) such as greeting cards
organize and generate a range of possible and at times conflicting desires that regulate and help individuals perform situated
activities and subjectivities. Although there are variations, generally, we typically recognize greeting cards (GCs) as folded cards
with some kind of illustration and message on the front, a brief
message on the inside sometimes written in rhyme (which usually remarks in some way on the front message and/or illustration), and a blank space for a more personal message from the
sender. The back of the card includes the name of its manufac-
turer, its price, as well as a bar-code. The GC is also fitted with an
envelope for delivery purposes. (More recent e-greeting cards
add multimedia and dispense with envelopes and so forth, but
they still organize a similar discursive and ideological space.)
Traditionally, GCs bear messages of goodwill and are used on
socially acknowledged special occasions, such as birthdays, holi-
days, anniversaries, and graduations. However, GCs have
recently come to be used on more commonplace occasions such
as a promotion at work, a retirement, or a move to a new city and
to exchange more everyday sentiments such as "thinking of
you," "thank you," "good luck," and so on. In fact, as we
observed in chapter 2, the cards now seem to sanction, and, in
turn, reproduce, the very occasions that call for their use in such
examples as the "secretaries' day card," "the bosses' day card,"

"the grandparents' day card," and so on. These cards not only respond to certain occasions; they also maintain these occasions as certain desires that their use helps fulfill.

Any serious examination of the GC will have to take into account its various subgenres. If we define genres as typified sites of action that at once elicit and reproduce recurrent situations by organizing and generating the desires, activities, subjectivities, and relations that take place within these situations, then we have to consider the possibility that a "humorous birthday card from a friend" is a different subgenre from an "anniversary card from a husband." In fact, the *"humorous* birthday card from a friend" would even have to be a different subgenre from the *"serious* birthday card from a friend," or, for that matter, the "serious birthday card from a *wife."* Each of these subgenres orchestrates a more specific site of action, engaging the sender and receiver in a specific textured economy with its own attachments, relations, subjectivities, and consequences.[10]

Whatever we wish to call this constellation of related subgenres and however finely we wish to distinguish them, what is of interest here are the various social relations and subject positions these sub-genres make possible to us as a culture. When an individual approaches a GC display, he or she is confronted with hundreds of choices: cards for various occasions and cards representing various social relations, including receiver and sender subjectivities. These situations and relations are labeled on the display stand. First, there are the overarching labels, indicating the occasion the card represents: birthday, anniversary, Mother's Day, Christmas, and so on. Below these labels are more specific distinctions, which represent various subject positions: friend, wife, husband, son, daughter, daughter-in-law, father, mother, lover, and so on. Although these positions generally refer to the recipients of the GC, they indirectly regulate the cultural positions that the senders assume as a result of engaging in this relationship with the receiver. If I choose, for example, a GC labeled as "wife," then I enter into this relationship in the role of husband. I might instead have chosen a card for a lover or friend, or a general one about age. Each would situate me in a different position of articulation. In each case, the GC has begun to reproduce larger cultural prescriptions as to who can engage in what relationships, when, and under what conditions. The occasions represented on the CG display, organized by subjectivities and relations, are largely indicative of what our culture sanctions as the potential social relations and identities we can assume on a given occasion, textually embodying the range of possible occasions, desires, relations, and subjectivities available to us. This GC-maintained motive potential informs the ideological superstructure which for Giddens defines the allowable sentimental intentions we can internalize and then enact. Subjects who do not find themselves represented in or who opt out of these subjectivities, desires, and relations will often have to enact their subjectivities in opposition to these formations.

An individual, of course, "chooses" from these various GC relations and subject positions. It is not uncommon, in fact, to find oneself lingering for lengthy periods of time before the array of desire-able subjectivities and relations trying to locate the card most suitable for one's particular situation and one's particular relation to the receiver. We struggle because we want to find the right card, the one that appropriately actualizes *our* relation to the receiver as well as *our* sense of who *we* imagine ourselves to be. Yet what we choose is always going to situate us within a discursive and ideological formation that frames who we are and how we relate to the receiver. We choose, that is, a subject position in the Althusserian sense of being interpellated. The GC does what an ideological apparatus does: it procures from individuals the "recognition that they really do occupy the place it designates for them as theirs in the world" (Althusser 1984, 52). It positions us as agents of the desires it elicits. So no matter what our "real" relation is to the receiver, that relationship becomes in part mediated by the socio-rhetorical environment of the card. Once chosen, the card becomes not merely a textured representation of its receiver, but rather situates the receiver within a desired subjectivity that is then invoked by the sender. At the same time, when we as senders write our personal message (PM—and not all senders write PMs), we too are being invoked by the card: the GC position we chose to occupy, the style of the card (humorous, somber, serious, playful), the relation established by the already existing message and illustration, etc. That is, the GC in which we write our PM is not some free, open space we use to communicate a message we invented beforehand; rather, it informs the nature of the relation between us as writers and the receiver as audience because to some extent both writer and audience positions are already partly defined by the card and its genre. Within what Freadman calls the "jurisdiction" (2002) of the genre, the PM becomes an "uptake" of the card's message and illustration.

Of course, PMs particularize the GC to our immediate circumstances. I have received cards in which part of the printed message was crossed out by the sender in an effort to make the card apply specifically to our relationship. Frequently, senders will write their PM in direct relation to the GC's message or illustration, extending the printed message or resisting it. But even this act of resistance is made possible by the situation of the card, which we identify with and/or rebel against in our uptake. An example of such identity construction and the possibility of resistance can be seen if we look at a line of Hallmark GCs. Called the "Mahogany" line, these cards are designed specifically for people of color in an effort, presumably, to include people of color in these commodified desires, subjectivities, and relations. Not surprisingly, these cards represent cultural stereotypes. For example, non-Mahogany GCs that offer congratulations for the birth of a child will commonly represent the birth of a child either as a solemn, blessed occasion or as an occasion for sleepless nights for the parents, great joy, and endless bottles and diapers. But rarely if ever would we find a card such as the following, from the Mahogany line, which describes the newborn African-American infant as "the pride of his race" and then admonishes his parents to instill "morals and values" into the child. In this case, individuals may resist the card in a number of ways, either by choosing not to purchase it, by choosing to write a letter of complaint to Hallmark, or by using the occasion of the card to comment on or subvert its racial assumptions in their PM to the receiver. Regardless of the form of resistance, however, the fact of the card remains as one more cultural formation of African-American identity. These cards not only embody the desires that inform their racialized assumptions, but they also position writers and readers of these cards within these desires, which organize and generate the choices writers make when they write in these genred spaces.

The fact that as writers we always confront representations of who we are and how we should behave whenever we write within a genre does not mean we do not or cannot contest them. We do. But, as I have been arguing, we do so not by escaping genre and entering some genre-free environment in which we can access some inherent identity. Rather, we do so in part by engaging other genres, which draw on other subject positions and desires. This way, our identity is always plural and always in the process of presencing as we are informed by desires which are reproduced and rhetorically actualized by the various genres we use every day. Ignoring the constitutive influence of these genres leaves teachers and scholars of writing with only a partial view of agency. And so a great deal of the invention techniques we research and teach begin with the writer. We teach heuristics such as freewriting, clustering, and brainstorming in order to help students discover and explore ideas to write about. Our overriding assumption continues to be that the writer is the locus of invention.

To argue that writers' intentions are also generated and organized by the genres they have available to them, however, is to posit genres, not just writers, as the locus of invention. Writers invent by locating themselves within genres, which function as habits as well as habitats for acting in language. Social workers, for example, must invent themselves within the genre of the assessment report as they are writing an assessment report. The assessment report, therefore, does not only provide social workers with a habitual way of using language; it is also a habitat for using language, a way of conceptualizing and enacting social work practices, desires, relations, and subjectivities—indeed, a way of *being* in the world as a social worker. In researching and teaching invention, we need to redirect our attention from the writer to the writer's social and rhetorical location in the world, the habitat in which the writer functions. In a way, as I described in the previous chapter, we need to return to a more rhetorical theory of invention, in which invention takes place, quite literally, within a place—what classical rhetoricians called the topoi or commonplaces. These conceptual and rhetorical places served as the general sites to which rhetors would turn to discover ideas and means of persuasion for any given situation. In this chapter, I have considered genres as such sites of invention, situated topoi within which writers invent themselves as well as their subjects. In the next chapter, I will examine how writers reposition themselves within sites of invention by looking at an environment that is coordinated by a set of genres, each of which embodies its own "topoi" or habitat—social activities, relations, subject positions, and rhetorical conventions for enacting these activities, relations, and positions—within the overall environment: the first-year writing classroom. Embodying and helping communicants to enact these habitats within the classroom, genres can teach us a great deal about why and how writers invent as they reposition themselves from one genre to another. The case I have tried to make in this chapter, that genres situate writers within positions of articulation, and the more detailed analysis I will provide in the next chapter lead me to argue, as I will in the final chapter, that we can and should teach students how to access and interrogate these genred positions of articulation so that students can participate in these positions more meaningfully and critically.

# 5

## SITES OF INVENTION
### *Genre and the Enactment of First-Year Writing*

Genres themselves form part of the discursive context
to which rhetors respond in their writing and, as such,
shape and enable the writing; it is in this way that form
is generative.

AVIVA FREEDMAN, "Situating Genre"

We need to be aware not only that genres are socially
constructed but also that they are socially constitutive—
in other words, that we both create and are created by
the genres in which we work.

THOMAS HELSCHER, "The Subject of Genre"

[A genre's discursive features] are united within the
relatively stable discursive "type" to offer us a form
within which we can locate ourselves as writers—that is,
a form which serves as a guide to invention,
arrangement, and stylistic choices in the act of writing.

JAMES F. SLEVIN, "Genre Theory, Academic<br>Discourse, and Writing in the Disciplines"

Reflecting on the concept of invention in the classical rhetorical tradition, Jim Corder writes that *"inventio,* by its nature, calls
for openness to the accumulated resources of the world a
speaker lives in, to its landscapes, its information, its ways of
thinking and feeling. . . . *Inventio* is the world the speaker lives
in" (1994, 109). Similarly, Sharon Crowley writes that "invention
reminds rhetors of their location within a cultural milieu that
determines what can and cannot be said or heard" (1990, 168).
Invention takes *place,* which is why classical rhetoricians recom-
mended the topoi or commonplaces as the sites in which
rhetors could locate the available means of persuasion for any

given situation. As heuristics for invention, the topoi were thus rhetorical habitats—"language-constituted regions" (Farrell 1996, 116) and "resources, seats, places, or haunts" (Lauer 1996, 724)—which framed communal knowledge and provided rhetors with shared methods of inquiry for navigating and participating in rhetorical situations. Invention, as such, was not so much an act of turning inward as it was an act of locating oneself socially, a way of participating in the shared desires, values, and meanings already existing in the world. As Scott Consigny explains, the topoi were both "the *instrument* with which the rhetor thinks and the *realm* in and about which he thinks" (1994, 65; my emphasis). The topoi helped rhetors locate themselves and participate within common situations.

In much the same way, genres are also instruments and realms—habits and habitats. Genres are the conceptual realms within which individuals recognize and experience situations at the same time as they are the rhetorical instruments by and through which individuals participate within and enact situations. The Patient Medical History Form, for example, not only conceptually frames the way the individual recognizes the situation of the doctor's office; it also helps position the individual into the figure of "patient" by providing him or her with the rhetorical habits for acting in this situation. Likewise, George Washington "invents" the first state of the union address by rhetorically situating himself within the conceptual realm of an antecedent genre, the "king's speech," which provides him not only with a way of recognizing the situation he is in, but also a way of rhetorically acting within it. And similarly, D. H. Lawrence is motivated to invent his autobiography differently as he perceives and enacts it within different genres. As such, why individuals are motivated to act and how they do so depends on the genres they are using. These genres serve as the typified and situated topoi within which individuals acquire, negotiate, and articulate desires, commitments, and methods of inquiry to help them act in a given situation, thereby inventing not only certain lines of argument (logos), but also certain subjectivities (ethos—think of the subject position Washington assumes when he writes the "king's speech) and certain ways of relating to others (pathos—think of the relation Washington sets up between himself and Congress, and, as a result, how Congress reacts to Washington).[1] Conceived thus, invention does not involve an introspective turn so much as it involves the process by which individuals locate themselves within and devise ways of rhetorically acting in various situations. In this way, invention is a process that is inseparable from genre since genre coordinates both how individuals recognize a situation as requiring certain actions and how they rhetorically act within it.

Genres, thus, are localized, textured sites of invention, the situated topoi in which communicants locate themselves conceptually *before* and rhetorically *as* they communicate. To begin to write is to locate oneself within these genres, to become habituated by their typified rhetorical conventions to recognize and enact situated desires, relations, practices, and subjectivities in certain ways. I will now consider one such genre-constituted environment within which teacher and students "invent" various situated practices, relations, and subjectivities as they (re)locate themselves from one genre-situated topoi to the next: the first-year writing course.

In *Modern Dogma and the Rhetoric of Assent*, Wayne Booth speculates on a theory of interaction and self-formation similar to the one I have been proposing in my discussion of genre and agency. "What happens," he wonders, "if we choose to begin with our knowledge that we are essentially creatures made in symbolic interchange, *created in the process of sharing intentions,* values, meanings? . . . What happens if we think of ourselves as essentially participants in a field or process or mode of being persons together?" (1974, 134; my emphasis). In this chapter, I will examine the first-year writing course from the perspective of Booth's question, describing and analyzing the first-year writing course as an activity system coordinated by a constellation of genres, each of which constitutes its own topoi within which teachers and students assume and enact a complex set of desires, relations, subjectivities, and practices. By investigating how teachers and students make their way through these genres, we can observe the complex relations and repositioning that teachers and students negotiate as they participate within and between genred discursive spaces. Invention takes place within and between these genred spaces, as one genre creates the timing and opportunity for another. When they write their essays, for example, students are expected to perform a discursive transaction in which they recontextualize the desires embedded in the writing prompt as their own self-sponsored desires in their essays. Invention takes place at this intersection between the acquisition and articulation of desire. By analyzing the syllabus, writing prompt, and student essay as genred sites of invention, I hope to shed light on how students and teachers reposition themselves as participants within these topoi at the same time as they enact the activity system we call the first-year writing course.

## THE FIRST-YEAR WRITING COURSE AND ITS GENRES

In the previous chapter, I discussed how a site of activity (for example, a physician's office) is coordinated by a variety of genres, referred to as "genre sets" (Devitt 1991) or "genre systems" (Bazerman 1994a), each genre within the set or system constituting its own site of action within which communicants instantiate and reproduce situated desires, practices, relations, and subjectivities. Within a site of acitvity, thus, we will encounter a constellation of related, even conflicting situations, organized and generated by various genres. David Russell, adapting Vygotsky's concept of activity theory to genre theory, has described this constellation of situations that make up an environment as an "activity system," which he defines as "any ongoing, object-directed, historically conditioned, dialectically structured, tool-mediated human interaction" (1997, 510). Examples of activity systems range from a family, to a religious organization, to a supermarket, to an advocacy group. As Russell defines it, an activity system resembles what Giddens calls "structure." Like structure, an activity system is constituted by a dialectic of agents or subjects, motives or social needs, and mediational means or tools (what Giddens refers to as "structurational properties"). Each element of the dialectic is constantly engaged in supporting the other, so that, for instance, agents enact motives using tools which in turn reproduce the motives that require agents to use these tools and so on. As Russell explains, "activity systems are not static, Parsonian social forces. Rather, they are dynamic systems constantly re-created through micro-level interactions" (512). In their situated, micro-level activities and interactions, discursively and ideologically embodied as genres, participants in an activity system are at work "operationalizing" and, in turn, reproducing the ideological and material conditions that make up the activity system within which they interact. Each genre enables individuals to enact a different situated activity within an activity system. Together, the various genres coordinate and synchronize the ways individuals define, interact within, and enact an activity system.

Russell's description of an activity system helps us conceptualize both how genres interact within a system of activity and how they help make that system possible by enabling individuals to participate within and in turn reproduce its related actions. The genres that constellate an activity system do not only organize and generate participants' activities within the system, however. They also, as Russell describes, link one activity system to another through the shared use of genres (1997; 2002). Participants in one activity system, for instance, use some genres to communicate with participants in other activity systems, thereby forming intra- and intergenre system relations. By applying the concept of activity system to school settings, especially to the interactions among micro-level disciplinary and administrative activity systems that together form the macro-level activity system of the university, Russell provides us with a model for analyzing the first-year writing course as one activity system within a larger activity system (the English department), within an even larger activity system (the College of Liberal Arts and Sciences), within an even larger activity system (the university), and so on. The constellation of genres within each of these related systems operationalizes the situated actions of participants within that system in order "to create stabilized-for-now structures of social action and identity" (Russell 1997, 514). The genres that coordinate each of the mirco-level activity systems within a macro-level activity system function interactively as a series of uptakes, with one genre creating an opportunity for another, as in the example of the Department of Defense, in which requests for proposals generate funding proposals, which generate contracts, which generate reports and experimental articles, and so on (520). At the same time, not everyone involved in an activity system is or needs to be engaged in all its genres. As Russell explains, "in a typical school, for example, the teacher writes the assignments; the students write the responses in classroom genres. The administrators write the grade form; the teachers fill it out. The parents and/or the government officials write the checks; the administrators write the receipts and the transcripts and report to regents" (520). In this scenario, the various participants (teachers, students, parents, administrators) are all involved in micro-level activity systems which interact in close proximity to one another and which together comprise the macro-level activity system called a school. In what follows, I will focus on one particular micro-level activity system within a college or university: the first-year writing course.

Like other college or university courses, the first-year writing (FYW) course takes place, for the most part, in a physical setting, a material, institutionalized site most often situated within a building on campus.[2] It is a place a teacher and students can physically enter and leave. But as in the case of the physician's office, the classroom is not only a material site; it is also a discursive site, one mediated and reproduced by the various genres its participants use to perform the desires, positions, relations, and activities that enact it. For example, one of the first ways that a classroom becomes a FYW course (or any other course for that matter) is through the genre of the syllabus, which, as I will describe shortly, organizes and generates the classroom as a textured site of action which locates teacher and students within a set of desires, commitments, relations, and subject positions. At the same time, the syllabus also manages the set of genres that will enable its users to enact these desires, relations, and subjectivities. In this way, the syllabus and its related FYW course genres orient teachers and students in a discursive and ideological scene of writing which locates them in various, sometimes simultaneous and conflicting positions of articulation. The choices teachers and students make in this scene emerge from, against, and in relation to these positions. As such, "the classroom is always invented, always constructed, always a matter of genre" (Bazerman 1994b, 26). When we only identify students as writers in the writing classroom, then, we are ignoring the extent to which teachers (as well as those who administer writing programs) are also writers of and in the writing classroom—writers of the genres that organize and generate them and their students within a dynamic, multitextured site of action. The FYW course, thus, is a site where writing is already at work to make writing possible. Seen in this light, the FYW course is not as artificial as some critics make it out to be. It may be artificial when, chameleon-like, it tries to mimic public, professional, or disciplinary settings, or when it tries to imagine a "real" external audience for student writing. But the classroom in its own right is a dynamic, textured site of action mediated by a range of complex written and spoken genres that constitute student-teacher positions, relations, and practices.[3] As they reposition themselves within and between these genres, teachers and students acquire, negotiate, and articulate different desires, which inform the choices they make as participants in the FYW course.

The set of written genres that coordinates the FYW course includes, but is not limited to, the course description, the syllabus, the course home page, student home pages, the grade book, the classroom discussion list, assignment prompts, student essays, the teacher's margin and end comments in response to student essays, peer workshop instructions, student journals or logs, peer review sheets, and student evaluations of the class. These "classroom genres" (Christie 1993; Russell 1997) constitute the various typified and situated topoi within which students and teacher recognize and enact their situated practices, relations, and subjectivities. I will now examine three of these classroom genres, the syllabus, the assignment prompt, and the student essay, in order to analyze how writers reposition and articulate themselves within these sites of invention. By doing so, I hope to demonstrate the extent to which, when they invent, writers locate themselves in a complex, multilayered set of discursive relations, so that by the time students begin to write their essays they do so in relation to the syllabus, the writing assignment, and the various other genres that have already located them and their teachers in an ideological and discursive system of activity.

*The Syllabus*

In many ways, the syllabus is the master classroom genre, in relation to which all other classroom genres, including the assignment prompt and the student essay, are "occluded" (Swales 1996). According to Swales, occluded genres are genres that operate behind the scenes and often out of more public sight, yet play a critical role in operationalizing the commitments and goals of the dominant genre, in this case, the syllabus. As such, the syllabus plays a major role in establishing the ideological and discursive environment of the course, generating *and* enforcing the subsequent relations, subject positions, and practices teacher and students will perform during the course. In some ways, the syllabus, like the architecture students' sketchbooks described in the previous chapter, functions as what Giltrow calls a "metagenre," an "atmosphere surrounding genres" (2002, 195) that sanctions and regulates their use within an activity system. It is not surprising, thus, that the syllabus is traditionally the first document students encounter upon entering the classroom. Immediately, the syllabus begins to transform the physical setting of the classroom into the discursive and ideological site of action in which students, teacher, and their work will assume certain significance and value. That is, within the syllabus, to paraphrase Giddens, the desires that inform the structure of the course become textually available to the students and teacher who then take up these desires as intentions to act. No doubt, the syllabus is a coercive genre, in the same way that all genres are coercive to some degree or another. It establishes the situated rules of conduct students and teacher will be expected to meet, including penalties for disobeying them. But even more than that, the syllabus also establishes a set of social relations and subjectivities that students and teacher have available to them in the course.

It is curious that, as significant a genre as it is, the syllabus has received so little critical attention (Baecker 1998, 61). In fact, to the extent that it is discussed at all, the syllabus is mostly described in "how to" guidebooks for novice teachers. For instance, both Erika Lindemann's *A Rhetoric for Writing Teachers* (1995) and Robert Connors and Cheryl Glenn's *The St. Martin's Guide to Teaching Writing* (1995) describe the syllabus in terms of its formal conventions, listing them in the order they most often appear: descriptive information such as course name and number, office hours, classroom location, significant phone numbers; textbook information; course description and objectives; course policy, including attendance policy, participation expectations, policy regarding late work, etc.; course requirements, including kinds and sequence of exams and writing assignments; grading procedures; any other university or departmental statements; and then a course calendar or schedule of assignments. In addition to presenting these conventions, Lindemann and Connors and Glenn also describe the purpose of the syllabus, acknowledging its contractual as well as pedagogical nature. Lindemann, for example, cites Joseph Ryan's explanation of the informational and pedagogical purposes of the syllabus:

> Students in the course use the syllabus to determine what it is they are to learn (course content), in what sense they are to learn it (behavioral objectives), when the material will be taught (schedule), how it will be taught (instructional procedures), when they will be required to demonstrate their learning (exam dates), and exactly how their learning will be assessed (evaluation) and their grade determined. (1995, 256–57)

In this sense, Lindemann claims that "syllabuses are intended primarily as information for students" (256).

Connors and Glenn, however, recognize the more political function of the syllabus. For them, "the syllabus, for all intents and purposes, is a contract between teacher and students. It states the responsibilities of the teacher and the students as well as the standards for the course" (1995, 10). The syllabus, then, informs the students and the teacher, protecting both from potential misunderstanding. It also informs the "structure of the class" by developing "a set of expectations and intentions for composition courses" (10–11). In other words, the syllabus establishes the course goals and assumptions as well as the means of enacting these goals and assumptions—both the structure of the course and the rhetorical means of instantiating that structure as situated practices. As Connors and Glenn remind teachers, the syllabus is "the first written expression of your personality that you will present to your students" (10).

Neither Lindemann nor Connors and Glenn, however, go on to analyze exactly how the syllabus locates teachers and students within this position of articulation or how it frames the discursive and ideological site of action in which teacher and students engage in coordinated commitments, relations, subjectivities, and practices. What effect, for instance, does the contractual nature of the syllabus have on the teacher-student relationship? What positions does the syllabus assign to students and teacher, and how do these positions get enacted and reproduced in the various situations and activities that constitute the FYW course? An analysis of the typified rhetorical features of the syllabus, especially its use of pronouns, future tense verbs, and abstract nominalizations, helps us begin to answer some of these questions.[4]

One of the more obvious characteristics of the syllabus is the way it positions students and teachers within situated subjectivities and relations. The student is frequently addressed as "you" ("This course will focus on introducing *you* to . . ."), as "students" ("*Students* will learn . . ." or "The goal of this course is to introduce *students* to . . ."), and as "we" ("*We* will focus on learning . . .") quite often interchangeably throughout the syllabus but at times even within the same section. For example, one teacher addresses her students in the "Course Objectives" section as follows: "Over the course of the semester, *you* will develop specific writing strategies which will help *you* adapt *your* writing skills to different contexts and audiences. Also, *we* will discuss how to approach and analyze the arguments of other writers, and how to either adapt or refute their views in *your* writing." This interchange between "you" and "we" on the pronoun level reflects a larger tension many teachers face when writing a syllabus: between establishing solidarity with students and demarcating lines of authority (Baecker 1998, 61). This tension is especially heightened in FYW courses which tend to be taught mostly by inexperienced teachers, most often graduate students who are themselves struggling with the tension between being teachers and students. Diann Baecker, drawing on Mühlhäusler and Harré's work (1990) on pronouns and social identity, applies this tension within pronouns to the social relations they make possible in the syllabus. Pronouns such as "you" and, in particular, "we" not only create social distinctions among communicants; they also "blur the distinction between power and solidarity and, in fact, allow power to be expressed as solidarity" (Baecker, 58).

It is perhaps this desire to mask power as solidarity that most characterizes the syllabus, a desire that teachers, as the writers of the syllabus, acquire, negotiate, and articulate. Positioned within this desire, the teacher tries to maintain the contractual nature of the syllabus while also invoking a sense of community. On the one hand, the teacher has to make explicit what the students will have to do to fulfill the course requirements, including the consequences for not doing so. On the other hand, the teacher also has to create a sense of community with the students so they can feel responsible for the work of learning. This balance is difficult, and, as we saw in the above example, many teachers will awkwardly fluctuate between "you" and "we" in order to maintain it. The following excerpt from another syllabus also reveals this fluctuation:

The goals of the course are two-fold. During the initial part of the semester, *we* will focus on learning to read critically—that is, how to analyze the writing of others. The skills that *you* will acquire while learning how to read an argument closely . . . will be the foundation for the writing *you* will do for the rest of the course. *Our* second objective . . .

This "we"/"you" tension reflects the balance the teacher is attempting to create between community and complicity. As Baecker explains, citing Mühlhäusler and Harré, "*we* is a rhetorical device that allows the speaker(s) to distance themselves from whatever is being said, thus making it more palatable because it appears to come from the group as a whole rather than from a particular individual" (1998, 59). The "we" construction tries to minimize the teacher's power implicit in the "you" construction by making it appear as though the students are more than merely passive recipients of the teacher's dictates; instead, they have ostensibly acquiesced consensually to the policies and activities described in the syllabus. The teacher, then, uses "you" and "we" in order to position students as subjects, so that without knowing it, they seem to have agreed to the conditions that they will be held accountable for. In this way, the syllabus is an effective contract, incorporating the student as other ("you") into the classroom community ("we") at the same time as it distinguishes the individual student from the collective. What the "you"/"we" construction seems to suggest is that "*we* as a class will encounter, be exposed to, and learn the following things, but *you* as a student are responsible for whether or not you succeed. *You* will do the work and be responsible for it, but *we* all agree what the work will be."

In her research, Baecker finds that "you" is by far the most common pronoun employed in syllabi (1998, 60), a finding supported by my own analysis. This "you," coupled with the occasional "we," the second most common pronoun, works as a hailing gesture, interpellating the individual who walks into the classroom as a student subject, one who then becomes part of the collective "we" that will operationalize this activity system we call the FYW course. As Mühlhäusler and Harré explain, it is "largely through pronouns and functionally equivalent indexing devices that responsibility for actions is taken by actors and assigned to them by others" (1990, 89). When a teacher identifies the student as "you," he or she is marking the student as the "other," the one on whom the work of the class will be performed: "You will encounter," "You will develop," "You will learn." But who exactly prescribes the action? Passive constructions such as the following are typical of the syllabus: "During the semester, *you* will be required to participate in class discussions," "*You* will be allowed a week to make your corrections." But who will be doing the requiring and the allowing? The teacher?

Not really. As much as the syllabus locates students within positions of articulation, it also positions the teacher within a position of articulation. The teacher's agency is seldom explicitly asserted through the first person singular; Baecker finds that "I" comprises an average of 24 percent of total pronoun usage per syllabus (1998, 60). More often, teachers mask their agency by using "we." Yet this "we" implicates the teacher into the collective identity of the goals, resources, materials, and policies of the course so that the teacher as agent of the syllabus becomes also an agent on behalf of the syllabus. The syllabus, in short, constructs its writer, the teacher, as an abstract nominalization in which the doer becomes the thing done. This is in part the genred subjectivity the teacher assumes when he or she writes the syllabus. For example, writers of syllabi rely on abstract nominalizations and nominal clauses to depict themselves as though they were the events and actions that they describe. Take, for instance, these typical examples: "Missing classes will negatively affect your participation grade," "Good class attendance will help you earn a good grade," "Acceptable excuses for missing a class include . . . ," "Each late appearance will be counted as an absence," "Guidance from texts constitutes another important component," "Writing is a process," "Conferences give us a chance to discuss the course and the assignments," "Plagiarism will not be tolerated." In these examples, we find objects, events, and actions that are incapable of acting by themselves treated as if they in fact are performing the actions. When a verb that conveys action in a sentence is transformed into a noun, we have the effect that somehow the action is performing itself—is its own subject, as in "missing classes" or "attendance." Rather than being the identifiable agents of the syllabus they write, teachers become part of the action they expect students to perform. This way, students come to see teachers less as prescribers of actions and more as guiding, observing, and evaluating student actions. As such, activities become substitutes for the agents who perform them, activities that teachers recognize and value and students subsequently enact.

The syllabus, therefore, is not merely informative; it is also, as all genres are, a site of action that produces subjects who desire to act in certain ideological and discursive ways. It establishes the habitat within which students and teachers rhetorically enact their situated relations, subjectivities, and activities. Both the teacher and the students become habituated by the genre of the syllabus into the abstract nouns that they will eventually perform. It is here, perhaps, that the syllabus's contractual nature is most evident, as it transforms the individuals involved into the sum of their actions, so that they can be described, quantified, and evaluated. No wonder, then, that the most dominant verb form used in the syllabus is the future tense, which indicates both permission and obligation, a sense that the activities and behaviors (the two become one in the syllabus) outlined in the syllabus are possible and binding. To be sure, the overwhelming number of future tense verbs present in the syllabus ("you will learn," "we will encounter") indicate that it is a genre that anticipates or predicts future action. Yet the discursive and ideological conditions it initially constitutes are already at work from day 1 to insure that these future actions will be realized.

The syllabus, in short, maintains and elicits the desires it helps its users fulfill. When a teacher writes the syllabus, he or she is not only communicating his or her desires for the course, but is also acquiring, negotiating, and articulating the desires already embedded in the syllabus. These desires constitute the exigencies to which the teacher rhetorically responds in the syllabus. For example, the contractual nature of the syllabus, especially the way it objectifies agency by constituting actors as actions which can then be more easily quantified and measured, is socio-rhetorically realized by such typified conventions as the "we"/"you" pronoun constructions, the abstract nominalizations, and the auxiliary "will" formations. By using these rhetorical conventions, the teacher internalizes the syllabus's institutional desires and enacts them as his or her intentions, intentions that he or she will expect students to respect and abide by. The teacher's intentions, therefore, are generated and organized rhetorically by the generic conventions of the syllabus. Teachers invent their classes, themselves, as well as their students by locating themselves within the situated topoi of the syllabus, which functions both as the rhetorical instrument and the conceptual realm in which the FYW course is recognized and enacted. Indeed, the syllabus, as Connors and Glenn warn teachers, *is* "the first expression of your personality," but the syllabus does not so much convey this a priori personality as it informs it.

The syllabus, then, helps establish the FYW course as a system of activity and also helps coordinate how its participants manage their way through and perform the various genres that operationalize this system, each of which constitutes its own site of invention within which teachers and students assume and enact a complex set of textured actions, relations, and subjectivities. Within this scene of writing, one such genre, the assignment (or writing) prompt, plays a critical role in constituting the teacher and student positions that shape and enable student writing.

## The Writing Prompt

While it does receive scholarly attention, mainly in handbooks for writing teachers such as Lindemann's (1995) and Connors and Glenn's (1995) (see also Murray 1989 and

Williams 1989), the writing prompt remains treated as essentially a transparent text, one that facilitates "communication between teacher and student" (Reiff and Middleton 1983, 263). As a genre, it is mainly treated as one more prewriting heuristic, helping or "prompting" student writers to discover something to write about. As Connors and Glenn describe it, "a good assignment . . . must be many things. Ideally, it should help students practice specific stylistic and organizational skills. It should also furnish enough data to give students an idea of where to start, and it should evoke a response that is the product of discovering more about those data. It should encourage students to do their best writing and should give the teacher her best chance to help" (1995, 58). Indeed, the most obvious purpose of the writing prompt is to do just that, prompt student writing by creating the occasion and the means for writing.

To treat the writing prompt merely as a conduit for communicating a subject matter from the teacher to the student, a way of "giving" students something to write about, however, is to overlook the extent to which the prompt situates student writers within a genred site of action in which students acquire and negotiate desires, subjectivities, commitments, and relations before they begin to write. The writing prompt not only *moves* the student writer to action; it also *cues* the student writer to enact a certain kind of action. This is why David Bartholomae insists that it is *within* the writing prompt that student writing begins, not *after* the prompt (1983). The prompt, like any other genre, organizes and generates the conditions within which individuals perform their activities. As such, we cannot simply locate the beginning of student writing in student writers and their texts. We must also locate these beginnings in the teachers' prompts, which constitute the situated topoi that the student writers enter into and participate within. As Bartholomae notes, a well-crafted assignment "presents not just a subject, but a way of imagining a subject as a subject, a discourse one can enter, and not as a thing that carries with it experiences or ideas that can be communicated" (1983, 306). This means that the prompt does not precede student writing by only presenting the student with a subject for further inquiry, a subject a student simply "takes up" in his or her writing, although that certainly is part of its purpose. More significantly, the prompt is a precondition for the existence of student writing, a means of habituating the students into the subject as well as the subjectivity they are being asked to explore so that they can then "invent" themselves and their subject matter within it.

As situated topoi, writing prompts are both rhetorical instruments and conceptual realms—habits and habitats. They conceptually locate students within a situation and provide them with the rhetorical means for acting within it. We notice examples of this in assignments that ask students to write "literacy narratives," narratives about their experiences with and attitudes relating to the acquisition of literacy. Teachers who assign them usually presume that these narratives give students the opportunity to access and reflect on their literacy experiences in ways that are transformative and empowering, ways that describe the challenges and rewards of acquiring literacy. What these assignments overlook, however, is that literacy narratives, like all genres, are not merely communicative tools; they actually reflect and reinscribe desires and assumptions about the inherent value and power of literacy. Students who are asked to write literacy narratives come up against a set of cultural expectations—embedded as part of the genre—about the transformative power of literacy as a necessary tool for success and achievement. Kirk Branch, for instance, describes how students in his reading and writing class at Rainier Community Learning Center struggled to invent themselves within the assumptions of these narratives. Aware of the social motives rhetorically embedded within these narratives, Branch explains, students wrote them as much to describe their experiences with literacy as to convince themselves and others of the transforming power of literacy. For example, commenting on one such student narrative, titled "Rosie's Story," Branch concludes,

"Rosie's Story" *writes itself* into a positive crescendo, a wave of enthusiasm which tries to drown out the self-doubt she reveals earlier. "Rosie's Story" does not suggest an unbridled confidence in the power of literacy to solve her problems, but by the end of the piece she drops the provisional "maybes" and "shoulds" and encourages herself to maintain her momentum: "Just keep it up." Her story, then, reads as an attempt to quash her self-doubt and to reassert the potential of literacy in her own life. (1998, 220; my emphasis)

In the end, it seems, the power of genre and the ideology it compels writers to sustain and articulate wins out. Rosie does not seem to be expressing some inherent intention as she writes this narrative. Rather, she seems to be locating herself within the desires embedded within the literacy narrative, desires that inform how she recognizes and performs herself in the situation of the reading and writing class. To claim, then, that her narrative begins *with* and *in* her is to overlook the extent to which she herself is being written by the genre she is writing.

We notice a remarkable example of how genres shape our perceptions and actions when Lee, a student in Branch's class, writes in his literacy narrative: "Furthermore Mr. Kirk gives us our assignments and he has always wanted us to do our best. He said, 'If you hadn't improved your English, you wouldn't have got a good job.' Therefore I worry about my English all the time" (Branch 1998, 221). "Does it matter," Branch wonders afterwards, "that I never said this to Lee?" (221) Apparently, Branch does not have to say it; Lee's assumption about literacy as a necessary tool for success is already rhetorically embedded in the genre of the literacy narrative as understood by the student, an assumption that Lee internalizes as his intention and enacts as his narrative when he writes this genre. It is within the situated topoi of the genre that Lee "invents" his narrative.

Often, teachers of writing overlook the socializing function of their writing prompts and consequently locate the beginnings of student writing too simply in the students rather than in the prompts themselves. What these teachers overlook—and writing teacher guides are no exception—is that students first have to situate and "invent" themselves in our prompts before they can assume the position of student writer. In fact, as we will discuss momentarily, it is the prompt that tacitly invokes the position that student writers are asked to assume when they write, so that students read their way into the position of writer via our prompts. Given this, it is perhaps more than a little ironic that most guides to writing effective assignment prompts emphasize the importance of specifying an audience *in* the prompt while more or less ignoring the students as audience *of* the prompt. As one of her five heuristics for designing writing assignments, for instance, Lindemann includes the following: *"For whom are students writing? Who is the audience? Do students have enough information to assume a role with respect to the audience? Is the role meaningful?"* (1995, 215). Here, the student is perceived only as potential writer to the audience we construct in the prompt. But what about the student as audience to the teacher's prompt, the position that the student first assumes before he or she begins to write? The assumption seems to be that the student exists a priori as a writer who has only to follow the instructions of the teacher's prompt rather than as a reader who is first invoked or interpellated into the position of writer by the teacher's prompt. This process of interpellation involves a moment of tacit recognition, in which the student first becomes aware of the position assigned to him or her and is consequently moved to act out that position as a writer.

The prompt is a genre whose explicit function is to make another genre, the student essay, possible. Within the FYW course activity system, it helps to create a timeliness and an opportunity for student writing in what Yates and Orlikowski, following Bazerman, refer to as "kairotic coordination" (2002, 110). In coordinating this interaction, the writing prompt functions to transform its writer (the teacher) and its readers (the students) into a reader (the teacher) and writers (the students). It positions the students and teacher into two simultaneous roles: the students as readers and writers, the teacher as writer and reader. First of all, the prompt rhetorically positions the teacher as both a writer and a reader. As he or she writes the prompt, the teacher positions him or herself as reader for the student text that the prompt will eventually make possible. The challenge that the prompt creates for the teacher is how to create the conditions that will allow students to recognize him or her not as the writer of the prompt, but as the eventual reader of their writing. That is, the teacher has to find a way to negotiate a double subject position, a subject subject, one who is doing the action (the subject as writer) and one on whom the action is done (the subject as reader). One way the teacher manages this double position is through a series of typified rhetorical moves and statements. For example, the following phrases are typical of prompts: "You should be sure to consider," "You probably realize by now that," "As you have probably guessed," "As you all know."[5] These are loaded phrases, because they not only offer suggestions the teacher-writer is giving to the student-readers; they also offer hints about what the teacher-writer will be expecting as a teacher-reader. When the teacher writes, "You probably realize by now that one effective way to support YOUR evaluation of those reviews is to offer examples from them in the way of quotes," he is telling the students something about him as an audience. He is basically saying, "Look, I care about using quotes to support evaluation, so if you want to write an effective evaluation for me, use quotes." Writing "one effective way" allows the teacher-writer to covertly express what he cares about as a reader. The next example is even more covert—and clever. After describing the assignment to the students, the teacher writes:

> To do this, *you should be able* to explain why the scene is central to the story's plot, what issues are being dealt with, and how or why the characters change. *The trick here* is to employ as many specific details from the story as possible. *You have the responsibility* to explain to your audience why you made the decision you did. (my emphasis)

The teacher who begins this prompt as a writer describing the assignment to the students as readers here begins to emerge as a

reader to the students as writers. "You should be able to" is a subtle, or perhaps not so subtle, way of letting students know what he
as a teacher-reader expects from their writing. "The trick here" is
even more effective, because it allows the teacher to enact the
role of reader while seeming to be an objective observer giving
helpful advice. In fact, however, there is no "trick" involved here,
just a calculated rhetorical way for the teacher to let students
know that he as a reader cares a great deal about the use of specific details. The only "trick" at work here is how the teacher creates the illusion that the writer addressing them is not the same
person as the reader who will be reading their writing. It is this
rhetorical sleight of hand that the prompt makes possible.

The prompt, therefore, allows the teacher to occupy two subject positions at once: writer/coach and reader/evaluator. As a
result, and at the same time, the prompt also constitutes the students as readers and writers. The students are prompted into
position or invoked as writers by the prompt, within which they
read and invent themselves. Indeed, every prompt has inscribed
within it a subject position for students to assume in order to
carry out the assignment. In FYW prompts, these roles can be
quite elaborate, asking students to pretend that "you have just
been hired as a student research assistant by a congressperson in
your home state" or "you have been asked by *Rolling Stone* to write
a critique of one of the following films." The prompts do not stop
here, however. They go on to specify to students how they should
enact these roles, as in the following example, in which the
teacher asks students to pretend that they are congressional aides:

> You must not explain what you "think" about this subject; the con-
> gressperson is more interested in the objective consideration of the
> issues themselves. And *of course*, you shouldn't recommend whether
> or not your employer should support the bill; *you are, after all, only
> an aide.* (my emphasis)

Words such as "of course," "obviously," "after all," "remember,"
and "certainly" all typically appear in prompts. Their function is
to establish shared assumptions; however, we have to question

just how shared these assumptions really are. How shared, for example, is the "of course" in the above example? Does the student-writer share this knowledge about congresspersons or is this a subtle way in which the prompt writer coerces complicity? The fact that the teacher-writer goes to the trouble of mentioning it suggests that perhaps the knowledge is not so obvious, that, in fact, "of course," "certainly," and "as we all know" are rhetorical means of presenting new information in the guise of old information (Pelkowski 1998, 7). If this is the case, then what we are witnessing is the prompt at work constituting the students as writers who assent to the ideology presented in the prompt, just as we saw in the case of the literacy narratives.

To a great extent, students have to accept the position(s) made available to them in the prompt if they are to carry out the assignment successfully. As all genres do, the prompt invites an uptake commensurate with its ideology, just as we saw in the example of the first state of the union address in which George Washington's choice of the "king's speech" prompted an appropriate congressional reply mirroring the echoing speeches of Parliament. While there is room for resistance, for students to refuse to accept the shared assumptions the prompt makes available to them, Pelkowski reminds us that "the power structure of the university denies students the ability to offer alternative interpretations of prompts. . . . Rather, an alternative interpretation of the assignment is not seen as such, but as a 'failure to respond to the assignment' (the F paper is often characterized in this way in statements of grading criteria)" (1998, 16). The writing prompt, in short, functions as a site of invention in which teacher and student create the conditions in which they will eventually interact as reader and writer.

The Student Essay

The very coercion masked as complicity that we observe in the syllabus and writing prompt is also at work when students begin to write their essays. This time, though, rather than being objects of this discursive move, students are expected to become its agents. In this way, students learn to enact the desires they acquire as participants within the FYW course and its system of genres. For example, one of the tricks teachers often expect students to perform in their writing involves recontextualizing the desires embedded in the writing prompt as their own self-generated desires. That is, students are expected to situate their writing within the writing prompt without acknowledging its presence explicitly in their writing so that it appears as though their writing created its own exigency, that somehow their writing is self-prompted. This rhetorical sleight of hand appears most visibly in the introductions of student essays, because it is there that students are asked to create the opportunity and timing for their essays in relation to the opportunity and timing as defined by the writing prompt. Experienced student writers know that they must negotiate this transaction between genres and do so with relative ease. Less experienced student writers, however, sometimes fail to recognize that the prompt and essay are related but separate genres, and their essays can frustrate teachers by citing the prompt explicitly in a way that shatters the illusion of self-sufficiency we desire students to create in their writing. In what follows, I will look at several examples of student essays to examine to what extent and how students negotiate this difficult transaction between genres as they function as agents on behalf of the prompt and agents of their own writing.

Yates and Orlikowski's work on the function of chronos and kairos in communicative interaction can help us interrogate the relation between the writing prompt and the student essay. They describe how genre systems choreograph interactions among participants and activities chronologically (by way of measurable, quantifiable, "objective" time) and kairotically (by way of constructing a sense of timeliness and opportunity in specific situations) within communities (2002, 108–10). In terms of chronos, the writing prompt assigns a specific time sequence for the production of the student essay, often delimiting what is due at what time and when. In this way, the writing prompt defines a chronological relationship between itself and the student essay. At the same time, however, the writing prompt also establishes the kairos for the student essay by providing it with a timeliness and an opportunity. In this way, the writing prompt defines a recognizable moment that authorizes the student essay's raison d'Être. Participating within this kairotic relationship between two genres, the student must, on the one hand, recognize the opportunity defined for him or her in the prompt and, on the other hand, reappropriate that opportunity as his or her own in the essay. Carolyn Miller describes this interaction as "the dynamic interplay between . . . opportunity as discerned and opportunity as defined" (1992, 312). Engaged in this interplay, the student writer must discern the opportunity granted by the prompt while writing an essay that seemingly defines its own opportunity. As such, the student writer needs to achieve and demonstrate a certain amount of generic dexterity, functioning within a genre system while masking its interplay. I will now look at some examples of how student writers negotiate this discursive transaction.

The following examples, from a FYW course, are all written in response to the same writing prompt. The students had read and discussed Clifford Geertz's "Deep Play: Notes on the Balinese Cockfight," had been assigned to take on the "role of 'cultural anthropologist' or 'ethnographer,'" had conducted some field observations, and were then prompted to write, "in the vein of Geertz in 'Deep Play,'" a

> claim-driven essay about the "focused gathering" [a term that Geertz uses] you observed. Your essay should be focused on and centered around what you find to be most significant and worth writing about in terms of the "focused gathering" you observed. . . . Some issues you might want to attend to include: How does the event define the community taking part in it? What does the event express about the beliefs of the community? What does the event say about the larger society?

Not only does the prompt assign students a subjectivity (the role of cultural anthropologist), but it also grants them an opportunity to transform their observations into an argument. In taking up this opportunity, the students perform a range of transactions between their essays and the writing prompt. Below, I will describe a sample of these transactions, starting with essays in which the writing prompt figures prominently (so that the coercion is visible) and concluding with essays in which the writing prompt is recontextualized as the student's own self-generated opportunity.

In those examples where students fail to enact the desired relationship between the prompt and the essay, the writing prompt figures explicitly in their essays, fracturing the illusion of autonomy that the essay, although prompted, tries to maintain. In the most obvious cases, such as the following, the student narrates explicitly the process of the essay's production:

> In my last literary endeavor [ostensibly referring to an earlier draft of the essay] I focused on one facet of the baseball game that I had gone to see. This time I am going to try to bring a few more topics to the table and focus on one thing in particular that I feel is significant.[6]

In this excerpt, the student appears to be narrating the prompt's instructions (stated as "be focused on and centered around what you find to be most significant") as he fulfills them. That is, he is telling us what he has been asked to do from one stage of the assignment sequence to the next as he does it, thereby making the coercion visible, as in the words, "This time I am going to try to . . ." Purposefully or not, the student in this case fails to perform the desired uptake between the prompt and his essay so that the prompt essentially speaks through him.

In a similar but less explicit way, the next essay also fails to reappropriate the prompt's defined opportunity as its own, so that the essay remains overly reliant on the prompt. The essay begins:

> Cultural events are focused gatherings that give observers insights to that certain culture. Geertz observes the Balinese culture and gains insights on how significant cockfighting is to the Balinese: including issues of disquieting and the symbolic meaning behind

the cockfights. My observations at a bubble tea shop in the International District also have similarities with Geertz's observations of the Balinese cockfight on the cultural aspect.

The phrases "cultural events" and "focused gatherings" locate the language of the prompt in the essay, but the first sentence simply rewords the language of the prompt rather than recontextualizing it as part of the essay's own constructed exigency. The question that would likely come to most teachers' minds, even though they already know the answer, would be, "So what? Why do we need to know this?" Similarly, in the second sentence, the only way to understand the relevance of the transition into Geertz is to know the prompt, which makes that connection. By the time the student describes her own observations in the third sentence, too much of the prompt's background knowledge is assumed, so that, for the logic of these opening sentences to work, a reader needs the prompt as context, yet this is the very relationship that the prompt and essay wish to downplay.

Compare the opening sentences of the above essay to the opening sentences of the following essay:

> When you want to know more about a certain society or culture what is the first thing that you need to do? You need to make and analyze detailed observations of that particular society or culture in its natural environment. From there you should be able to come up with a rough idea of "why" that particular culture or society operates the way it does. That's exactly what Clifford Geertz did. He went to Bali to study the Balinese culture as an observer.

As in the earlier example, this excerpt borrows the language of the prompt, but rather than rewording that language, it reappropriates it. This time, the reader meets Geertz on the essay's terms, after the student has provided a context for why Geertz would have done what he did. The same exigency that motivated Geertz becomes the student's exigency for writing his essay. Crude as it might be, the question that begins the essay performs the sleight of hand I described earlier, in which the student recontextualizes the question the prompt asks of him and asks it of his readers as if this is the question *he* desires to ask. In this way, the student becomes an agent of the agency at work on him. The student, however, seems unable or unwilling to sustain this uptake, for in the very next paragraph, he fractures the illusion he has begun to create. He writes:

> A couple of weeks ago I decided to go visit some friends in Long Beach Washington. Since it was something different from the norm of people in my class analyzing concerts and baseball games I decided to do my paper on Long Beach. I didn't have to look far for a cultural event to observe because the little ocean-side town was having a parade. . . . I pretty much took the Geertz approach and just tried to figure out what was going on.

Here, the student not only slips out of his assigned role as a "cultural anthropologist" by acknowledging his position as a student, along with other students writing a paper for class, but he also makes visible the coercion that prompted his essay when he writes that it did not take him long to find a cultural event to observe. Suddenly, he identifies himself as someone who has been prompted to find an event. At the same time, although he does refer to Geertz in the previous paragraph, the student's statement, "I pretty much took the Geertz approach," appears to be addressed to a reader who knows more than what the student has already explained about Geertz. That is, the statement imagines a reader who is familiar with the prompt that directed the student to take the Geertz approach in the first place. After all, the prompt asks students to write an essay "in the vein of Geertz."

In the previous example, we witness a student who begins to negotiate but does not quite sustain the complex interplay between the genred discursive spaces of the writing prompt and the student essay. In the next couple of examples, we observe students who manage this discursive transaction by recontextualizing the desires embedded in the prompt as their own seemingly self-prompted desires to write.

The following student begins her essay by describing the activities and interactions that typically occur at her church, thereby performing her role as a cultural anthropologist. Her third paragraph, which follows two paragraphs of observations, marks a transition. She writes:

> What purpose does all this serve? Geertz states in Deep Play: Notes on the Balinese Cockfight, "the cockfight is a means of expression." (Geertz pg. 420) In much the same way the Inn [the name of the church] is the same thing. It is a gathering for college aged people to express their faith in God.

By asking, "What purpose does all this serve?" this student asks the question that the prompt asks of her. In so doing, she makes it appear as though the inquiry that follows stems from her own curiosity. In the context of this appropriation, Geertz is not so much a figure she inherits from the prompt as he is a figure she invokes to create an opportunity for her essay to analyze the significance of the Inn. The student recontextualizes the opportunity as well as the authority from the discursive space of the prompt to the discursive space of the essay.

The next student performs a similar uptake, and does so with greater elegance. The student begins her essay by describing underground hip-hop music and the function it serves for its listeners, and then poses the question: "Is music created from culture, or is culture created from music?" The second paragraph begins to compare hip-hop to symphonies. The student writes:

> On a different note, a symphonic band concert creates a congregation of different status people uniting to listen to a type of music they all enjoy. "Erving Goffman has called *this* a type of 'focused gathering'—a set of persons engrossed in a common flow of activity and relating to one another in terms of that flow." (Geertz 405) This type of "focused gathering" is an example of music created from culture. "Focused gatherings" provide different emotions according to preference. The flocking of similar interests in the form of "focused gatherings" makes up a culture. Similar values are

shared to create one group of equals producing music for the same reason." (my emphasis)

By posing the question, "Is music created from culture, or is culture created from music?" the student creates an opportunity for her essay rather than inheriting that opportunity from the prompt. This is the question the *student* is asking. In the above excerpt, the student does not rely on the prompt's authority to justify the claim that "a symphonic band concert creates a congregation of different status people uniting to listen to a type of music they all enjoy." Instead, she appropriates the authority the prompt grants her to assert this claim. Only in the context of her authority does Geertz then figure into the essay. Notice how cleverly the student uses the quotation from Geertz to make it appear as though his description of a "focused gathering" was meant to define her focused gathering, the symphonic band concert. The determiner "this" no longer modifies the cockfight as Geertz meant it to; instead, it refers back to the concert, which is the student's subject of inquiry. In a way, this move creates the impression that the student found Geertz rather than having been assigned to use Geertz. There is very little evidence of prompting here.

In the remainder of the above excerpt, the student appears to perform what Fuller and Lee have described as an interiorized uptake, in which the student becomes positioned, through her interaction with the writing prompt, as a desiring subject who speaks from that subjectivity (2002, 222). In this case, the student internalizes the authority embedded in the prompt as her own authority in statements such as, "The flocking of similar interests in the form of 'focused gatherings' makes up a culture. Similar values are shared to create one group of equals producing music for the same reason." The student has appropriated the subjectivity assigned to her and now speaks from that position as a "cultural anthropologist." Fuller and Lee refer to this process of negotiation as "textual collusion," a term they use to describe how writers and readers move "around inside relations of power" (215). More so than her peers, this student seems able to negotiate the textured relations between the prompt and the essay, repositioning herself in the interplay between genred spaces so that she becomes an agent of the agency at work on her.

Invention takes place at the intersection between the acquisition and articulation of desire. When teachers assign students a writing prompt, they position students at this intersection so that part of what students do when they invent their essays involves recontextualizing the desires they have acquired as their own self-prompted desires to write. As such, teachers expect students to manage the interplay between coercion and complicity that we saw teachers perform in the syllabus (manifested in the "you" and "we" formations). Not all students, as we see in the above examples, are able to perform this sleight of hand with the same dexterity. And the reason for this, I would argue, has partly to do with the fact that some students do not know that this transaction requires them to move around between two genred sites of action, each with its own situated desires, relations, subjectivities, and practices—in short, its own positions of articulation. When they conflate these two worlds, students not only fracture the illusion of self-sufficiency the essay desires them to maintain, but students also fail to reposition their subjectivity and their subject matter within the discursive and ideological space of the essay. One way teachers can help students reposition themselves within such spheres of agency is to make genres analytically visible to students so that students can participate within and negotiate them more meaningfully and critically. In the next chapter, I will delineate my argument for such an explicit genre-based writing pedagogy.

## SUMMARY

Writing involves a process of learning to adapt, ideologically and discursively, to various situations via the genres that coordinate them. Writing is not only a skill, but a way of being and acting in the world in a particular time and place in relation to others.

The FYW course bears this out. As an activity system, it is sustained and coordinated by its various genres. Teachers and students assume ways of being and acting in the classroom not only because of its material setting—although that certainly does play a major part (see Reynolds 1998)—but also because of its multitextured sites of action as they are embodied within and between genres. As such, the writing that students do in the FYW course does not just begin with them by virtue of their being (enrolled) in this setting; it begins, rather, in the textured topoi that are already in place, shaping and enabling the writing that students as well as teachers do. As such, the environment of the classroom— or any other environment for that matter, including the doctor's office—is not only an ontological fact, but also a generic fact. It exists largely because we reproduce it in our genres, each of which constitutes a different but related topoi within which students and teacher function, interact, and enact subjectivities and practices. Since we reproduce the FYW course in the ways we articulate it, there is really little that is artificial or arbitrary about it, at least not in the way that Paul Heilker describes the FYW course as being artificial:

> Writing teachers need to relocate the *where* of composition instruction outside the academic classroom because the classroom does not and cannot offer students real rhetorical situations in which to understand writing as social action. (1997, 71)

Part of my argument in this chapter is that the FYW course *is* a "real rhetorical situation," one made up of various scenarios within which students (and their teachers) recognize one another, reposition themselves, interact, and enact their situated practices in complex social and rhetorical frameworks. Once we recognize this, once we acknowledge that the FYW course, like any activity system, is "not a container for actions or texts" but "an ongoing accomplishment" (Russell 1997, 513), we are on our way to treating the FYW course as a complex and dynamic scene of writing, one in which students can not only learn how to write, but, as we will discuss in the next chapter, can also learn what it means to write: what writing does and how it positions writers within systems of activity. Participating in the textual dynamics of the FYW course is as "real" a form of social action and interaction as any other textual practice.

As we have observed throughout the last two chapters in such genres as the PMHF, the social workers' assessment report, the résumé, the course journal, the "king's speech," the greeting card, the syllabus, the writing prompt, and the student essay, genres position their users to perform certain situated activities by generating and organizing certain desires and subjectivities. These desires and subjectivities are embedded within and prompted by genres, which elicit the various, sometimes conflicting, intentions we perform within and between situations. To assume that the writer is the primary locus of invention, then, is to overlook the constitutive power of genre in shaping and enabling how writers recognize and participate in sites of action.

Rather than being defined as the agency of the writer, invention is more a way that writers locate themselves, via genres, within various positions and activities. Invention is thus a process in which writers act as they are acted upon. The Patient Medical History Form is a case in point. So are the examples of George Washington and the first state of the union address, the example of the social workers' assessment report, and the example of the student essay in relation to the assignment prompt. All these examples point to the fact that there is more at work in prompting discourse than simply the writer's private intentions or even, for that matter, the demands of the writer's immediate exigencies. After all, George Washington responded to the exigencies of an unprecedented rhetorical situation not by inventing something new, but by turning to an antecedent genre, the "king's speech," which carried with it a rhetorical form of social action very much at odds with his more immediate exigencies. The available genre, rhetorically embodying social motives so powerful as to override the inspired democratic moment at hand, not only shaped the way Washington recognized and acted within his rhetorical situation, but the way Congress did too.

We notice a similar phenomenon at work in the example of the writing prompt. The writing prompt does not merely provide students with a set of instructions. Rather, it organizes and generates the discursive and ideological conditions which students take up and recontextualize as they write their essays. As such, it habituates students into the subjectivities they are asked to assume as well as enact—the subjectivities required to explore their subjects. By expanding the sphere of agency in which the writer participates, we in composition studies can offer both a richer view of the writer as well as a more comprehensive account of how and why writers makes the choices they do. As I will argue in the next chapter, teaching invention as a process in which writers access and locate themselves critically within genres not only can enrich the teaching of writing, but can also better justify the place and purpose of FYW courses in postsecondary education.

# 6

## RE-PLACING INVENTION IN COMPOSITION
### *Reflections and Implications*

It is strange that in institutions where every other
department represents the well-garnered scholarship
of the ages, in this department alone it should so often
be thought enough to put a pen into the student's
hand and say, as the angel said to John, "Write." . . . It
is strange indeed if we, as teachers of rhetoric, have
nothing higher to do than to correct bad spelling and
clean up slovenly sentences.

JOHN GENUNG, "The Study of Rhetoric in the
College Course"

An educational process in an important sense is a
process of initiation: an initiation, that is, into the ways
of working, or of behaving, or of thinking . . . particular
to one's cultural traditions. . . . Learning the genres of
one's culture is both part of entering into it with understanding, and part of developing the necessary ability
to change it.

FRANCES CHRISTIE, "Genres as Choice"

So far, I have argued that genres maintain the desires they
help writers to fulfill, and I have analyzed how, through genres,
writers position themselves within, negotiate, and articulate
these desires as recognizable, meaningful, consequential
actions. Because they situate writers within such positions of
articulation, genres, when analyzed, contribute to our understanding of how and why writers invent—how, that is, writers participate in and become agents of the agency at work on them
when they write. In previous chapters, I have examined genres
in this way, as sites of invention. In this chapter, I speculate on

what it would mean to apply this view of genre and invention to writing instruction, especially first-year writing courses. In particular, I argue that teachers can and should teach students how to identify and analyze genred positions of articulation so that students can locate themselves and begin to participate within these positions more meaningfully, critically, and dexterously. Genre analysis can make visible to students the desires embedded within genres; and by giving students access to these desires, we enable them to interrogate, enact, and reflect on the relations, subjectivities, and practices these desires underwrite. In what follows, I will describe what such a genre-based writing pedagogy might look like and how, by practicing it, we can re-imagine and justify the function and place of first-year writing instruction in the university.

## FIRST-YEAR WRITING AND THE PLACE OF COMPOSITION

John Genung wrote the words I cite in the above epigraph in 1887 (reprinted in Brereton 1995). The department to which he was referring was the newly founded Department of English and the course is what we now commonly recognize as first-year composition or first-year writing (FYW). I cite these words not to reflect on their antiquatedness, but to acknowledge the extent to which today, nearly a hundred and fifty years after its inception, scholars and teachers in composition studies can still look at the FYW course with the same bewilderment Genung did in 1887. We may not be as devoted today to correcting bad spelling and cleaning up slovenly sentences, but we are as much at a loss in articulating the goals of the FYW course as were its first teachers. As I was first drafting this chapter, in fact, administrators, teachers, and scholars of writing were heatedly debating on the Writing Program Administrators discussion list (WPA-L) the recommendations outlined in the most recent outcomes statement for FYW courses. As this listserv discussion and countless other exchanges at our conferences and in our journals suggest, those involved in the teaching and administration of the FYW course still struggle to agree on what the course outcomes ought to be and how best to achieve them. The course continues to have little to no disciplinary identity: its goals undefined, its place in the English department marginal at best, and its relationship to writing in the disciplines (WID) programs uncertain. Yet the course remains the most frequently taught in U.S. colleges and universities, and one of the few that carries a universal requirement. And despite the fact that some universities are beginning to consider making the course an elective rather than a requirement, and some composition programs have begun to separate from English departments to form departments of their own, the FYW course is not likely to disappear anytime soon.

Among the various and often contradictory rationales its advocates have advanced over the years for justifying the composition requirement, Sharon Crowley lists the following: to develop taste in students, to improve their formal and mechanical correctness, to provide them with a liberal education, to prepare them for their professions, to develop their personalities and "personal voices," to help them participate as able democratic citizens, to teach them textual analysis, to encourage them to become more critical thinkers, to introduce them to the composing process, to introduce them to academic disciplines and discourses, and, more recently, to encourage them to critique dominant cultural ideologies and to resist systems of oppression (1998, 6). Clearly, the course can try to do everything and end up, as its critics argue, doing very little. If there is, however, one goal upon which most writing teachers, university faculty, administrators, and the public can agree today, it continues to be that the course ought to teach students how to "master grammar, usage, and formal fluency" (Crowley 1998, 7). We ought to wonder, though, along with John Genung, why we cannot aspire to a higher goal.

Due in part to its undefined goals, the universally required FYW course, a mainstay of English departments and a tenuous part of their identity for a little more than a hundred years, has recently come under more scrutiny than ever before by those, especially within composition studies, who question its place and its purpose. Victor Vitanza (1999) and Susan Miller (1997) have questioned the "cultural studies" turn the course has taken at many universities, claiming that such a turn shifts the course's emphasis from the production of texts to their interpretation, a hermeneutic search for cultural and textual meanings more befitting the work of literary studies than composition. Rhetoric, these critics argue, is not a spectator sport. Even more recently, Sharon Crowley (2000; see also 1995) and others have begun to question why the course should remain a universal requirement in most U.S. colleges and universities, arguing in part that the course's requirement has not only stifled WID initiatives, but has also contributed to the exploitation of lecturers, graduate teaching assistants, and other part-time instructors who regularly teach it.

Perhaps the most serious challenges to the FYW course, however, have been those that question its place in the teaching of writing. Linda Bergmann (1996), Charles Hill and Lauren Resnick (1995), Carl Lovitt and Art Young (1997), Elaine Maimon (1983), David Russell (1991), and others argue, for instance, that the course does not prepare students for the disciplinary writing skills they need in their majors and careers, suggesting that "what students learn about writing in composition courses . . . is how to write in composition courses" (Bacon 2000, 590). Carl Lovitt and Art Young describe how, as more and more colleges and universities require writing-intensive courses across the curriculum and in the disciplines, English departments face increasing pressure to justify the FYW course, especially since the "overly restrictive conceptions of first-year composition courses have, in many instances, undermined the ability of such courses to contribute to the goals of university-wide writing programs" (1997, 113). Critics of the required writing course question whether a course housed in the English department and taught and administered mainly by English department faculty, part-time instructors, and graduate students can truly meet the discipline-specific rhetorical needs of the university and the professions. These critics wonder if writing skills are as transferable as we once thought they were—indeed, whether we can even talk about "good writing" outside of its social and rhetorical contexts. They also question the course's accountability, in particular, whose interests are being served by the universal requirement. These critics may have reason to be suspicious. As Linda Bergmann explains, once we in English departments "have the students safely registered in our classes, we teach them, deliberately or not, consciously or not, the things we really consider important: the standards, values, and conventions of our *own* disciplinary discourse" (1996, 58; Bergmann's emphasis). Such criticism, as well as recent movements to relocate writing programs outside of English departments, suggests that the FYW course has reached a critical impasse in its history. In response, we who study, teach, and administer it must address the course's responsibility to the university, especially its relationship to WID, as well as its location within the Department of English if we are to justify its continued existence.

In this chapter, I offer a genre-based approach to FYW instruction as a way to address the course's responsibility to WID and to justify its location within English. Such an approach, as I will argue, requires us to re-place invention from the writer to the genred sites of action in which the writer participates. This move calls for a rhetorical view of invention, one that builds on and adds to the work of Richard Young, Janice Lauer, and those who have followed them over the last forty years (see chapter 3). But despite such work, rhetoric (and an understanding of invention based on it) remains marginalized in writing instruction. This is not surprising given the history of FYW instruction. After all, the FYW course emerged at about the same time as the English department did, which was also at about the same time that rhetoric, a cross-disciplinary course of study, began to lose its stature in the new American university. The complicated history of the required writing course and its relationship to English studies and the new university has already been told at length by historians such as James Berlin (1987), John Brereton (1995), Robert Connors (1997), Sharon Crowley (1998), Susan Miller (1991), and Thomas Miller

(1997), and I do not pretend to retell it here. In what follows, I only wish to highlight how the displacement of rhetoric by composition within English departments may have contributed to the present impasse in FYW instruction and to describe how a genre-based understanding of invention might help us work through this impasse. As I argued in earlier chapters, by locating invention within genred sites of action, we treat invention rhetorically, as a way of being and acting in the world in relation to others within certain circumstances. And when we teach invention in this way, we teach students how to locate themselves within and participate in the textured worlds that surround them, within and beyond the academic disciplines. This genre-based approach to invention can connect FYW courses with WID in productive ways, ways that can help justify the function of FYW and its place within English departments.

## RHETORIC *AND* COMPOSITION?

It is common for us today to refer to "rhet-comp" as an academic discipline, but this label might actually hide some of the tensions between rhetoric and composition, tensions that first emerged about the time when the FYW course was established in American universities in the late nineteenth century. Historians have described various factors that accounted for the emergence of what came to be known as freshman English in the period between 1870 and 1900, among them, a gradual shift from orality to literacy; a concomitant interest in belletristic writing, especially written in the vernacular; a dramatic increase in the number of students as a result of the Morrill Act of 1862, which introduced masses of new students to the newly created state universities; the first American literacy crises in the late 1880s; and the influence of the German university system, which served as a model for the specialized, elective-based, research-oriented, and disciplinary nature of the new American university (Berlin 1987; Brereton 1995; Connors 1997). All these factors conspired to create the conditions for the FYW course. As Robert Connors explains, rhetoric, which had enjoyed nearly two thousand five hundred years of power and prestige as an academic field of study, could not survive under the conditions that saw the new American universities displace the traditional colleges. For one thing, the German universities, which trained so many of the Ph.D.'s who eventually returned to establish the new American universities, did not offer advanced degrees in rhetoric. Those who studied in Germany returned social scientists, chemists, psychologists, mathematicians, and philologists, but not rhetoricians (Connors 1997, 178–80). The advanced, research-based rhetorical training needed to sustain rhetoric as a discipline in the new American universities was not available. In addition, the German model was detail-oriented and empirical. Rhetoric, however, is more an art than a science, so it fared badly, eventually becoming displaced by philology—which involved more empirical analysis of the development and structure of languages—as the main research focus of English studies (Connors 1997, 178). It was philology, not rhetoric, that provided the theoretical and pedagogical underpinnings for the creation of the English department within which "freshman composition" developed.

In writing instruction, the shift in focus from production to product, from invention to arrangement, mirrored the displacement of rhetoric by philology within English studies. The English department built its research program around textual interpretation, not production, thereby marginalizing the teaching of how and why texts come to be and privileging the finished product as a timeless, fixed, even spiritual entity full of meanings to be scrutinized and deciphered (S. Miller 1991, 21–22). With the displacement of invention and the turn toward interpretation within English studies, rhetoric slowly lost its place within the English department. Aided by the influence of Hugh Blair's *Lectures on Rhetoric and Belles Lettres* (first published in 1783), newly minted English scholars transformed rhetoric into criticism (T. Miller 1997, 227), a transformation we recognize to this day. In this context, rhetoric as a four-year course of study was displaced by composition as a required, freshman-level, two semester course (Brereton 1995, 13), so that between 1865 and 1900 the new American university transformed from "an intensely rhetorical world" (Connors 1997, 9) with rhetorical study not only a part of the curriculum but also a part of students' extracurricular activities to a "diverse, large, fragmented university organized by academic disciplines" (Brereton 1995, 3–4). Within this new university culture, rhetoric, interdisciplinary by nature, could not be sustained as a central activity. As Connors explains, "it had no real place in the new universities, and its fall correlates exactly with their rise" (1997, 178).

The move from rhetoric to composition was marked not only by a shift from speaking to writing, but also by a shift from a civic to an interiorized subjectivity (Connors 1997, 44). In writing courses, this move from "objective, centripetal writing tasks to subjective, centrifugal tasks" (Connors 1997, 296), what Thomas Miller has described as a move toward "a tasteful self-restraint and a disinterested perspective on experience" (1997, 43), was reflected in the "essay of manners and taste," which became the genred site for the formation and enactment of a bourgeois subjectivity characterized "by the disinterested perspective of the critical commentator whose personal character is revealed in a polished style, restrained sense of polite decorum, and critical attention to how gestures and expressions reveal individuals' sensibility" (T. Miller 1997, 47). Against the backdrop of this interiorized perspective, informed by romantic theories of genius and originality as well as the "philological and exegetical traditions that emphasized the autonomous writer and the text as individually held intellectual property" (Lunsford and Ede 1994, 420), the writer's subjectivity became and, as I argued in chapter 3, largely continues to be the subject of writing instruction.

What remains constant over the nearly 150-year history of the FYW course, a time during which composition displaced rhetoric as the guiding principle, is that writing came more and more to describe a process of learning (about oneself, one's experiences, one's subject, one's world) rather than a process of being and acting in the world.[1] This move from writing as rhetoric to writing as composition—what Thomas Cole describes as the rise of the "expressionistic notion of the uniquely adequate verbalization of a unique idea" (1991, 21)—has had a great deal to do with the modern decline of rhetoric. It has also, as I have suggested above, had a great deal to do with the ascent of the writer, so much so that we could profitably argue that the composition course as we know it today exists first and foremost not to introduce students to the ways of academic discourse (which is how some teachers and administrators of the course advertise its mission) but to develop and articulate the writing self, what Francis Christie has described as "the concern for the individual, and for the development of that individual, confident of opinion, capable of independence of action and of self expression" that has so long occupied the responsibility of English teachers (1988, 23).

And so, as Susan Miller describes, the FYW course and the process movement that largely informs it continue to "focus on the author/writer, not on the results of authorship or of writing" (1991, 98). That is, many teachers of the course continue to ignore the social and rhetorical effects of writing, not only on its audience but on its writers as well. As I have been arguing, though, writers are always affected by and affect the conditions in which they write, especially as these conditions are discursively embodied by genres—acting as they are acted upon by the genres they write. Within genre, the writer rhetorically acquires certain desires and subjectivities, relates to others in certain ways, and enacts certain actions. Genres, in short, rhetorically place their writers in specific conditions of production. It is within these conditions of production, within genres, that invention takes place. By redirecting the trajectory of the writer's inquiry from the self to the rhetorical conditions within which the self is constituted, this view of invention challenges us to rethink why and how we teach FYW. Essentially, it asks us to take more of a rhetorical than a process-based approach in FYW, one in which students are encouraged to look outward, at how already existing discursive and ideological formations such as genres coordinate ways of thinking and acting in different disciplinary contexts, ways that student writers can interrogate, adopt, and eventually learn to enact and/or resist when they write. The primary goal of such a FYW course would be to teach students how to locate themselves and their activities meaningfully and critically within these genred positions of articulation. Such a rhetorical view of invention, I argue, allows us to justify FYW as a site in which students can begin to learn how to navigate disciplinary contexts rhetorically, thus forging real links to WID rather than consciously or unconsciously serving mainly the aspirations of English departments. By teaching students that invention is as much a public as it is a private act (an act of [re]positioning as much as of expressing oneself), we teach them how to make visible for themselves and to practice in their writing the rhetorical habits that inform the disciplinary and professional habitats within which they will function. It is in this ability to teach students how to locate and invent themselves rhetorically within various sites of action (a rhetorical, metacognitive literacy)—an ability to heighten awareness of disciplinarity and rhetoric—that the future of FYW is most promising and justified.

## RETHINKING WRITING INSTRUCTION: AN ARGUMENT FOR A GENRE-BASED APPROACH TO FYW

The WID movement for years has been promoting and developing discipline-specific writing research and instruction, research and instruction rooted in the ideological and discursive contexts of various disciplines within the university. This movement, reflecting research into the social bases of writing, suggests that we need to teach writing in its disciplinary and professional contexts, where writing is not only a means of communication—the acquisition of certain communicative skills—but also a means of socialization into disciplinary values, assumptions, relations, and practices. Such research raises questions about the efficacy of FYW and its focus on general writing skills. Yet rather than considering this move toward disciplinary writing as a threat to the existence of FYW, I think we as scholars, administrators, and teachers of the course ought to embrace this movement as an opportunity for us not only to justify FYW, but also to rethink its purpose and its place. FYW does not need to stand as an alternative to or in opposition to WID. As Charles Hill and Lauren Resnick rightfully maintain, it is nearly impossible to re-create disciplinary conditions in the FYW course, but this should not mean, as Hill and Resnick go on to suggest, that the course "can do little to prepare students for writing within the various professional contexts they will be entering after graduation" (1995, 146). The fact that the FYW course cannot re-create the various ideological and discursive formations that underwrite disciplinary and professional contexts does *not* mean that the FYW course cannot prepare students for writing within these contexts. It can. By functioning as a kind of rhetorical promontory from which we teach students how to read and negotiate the boundaries of various disciplinary and professional contexts, the FYW course can become the site in which students learn how to access, interrogate, and (re)position themselves as writers within these disciplinary and professional contexts. In this way, FYW can function as a complement, perhaps even as a prerequisite, to WID, a site within the structure of the university that enables students to reflect critically on and at the same time to write about the university's disciplinary structures.[2] Genres, I argue, can serve as the "passports" for accessing, analyzing, navigating, and participating in these disciplinary structures.

At the end of *Textual Carnivals*, Susan Miller suggests that as teachers and scholars of writing, we need to be "disclosing connections between specific social and textual superstructures and highlighting how writing situations construct their participant writers before, during, and after they undertake any piece of writing" (1991, 198). I agree that this should be a primary goal of FYW, and a genre-based writing pedagogy can help us achieve it. As discursive and ideological formations, genres allow teachers and students to examine the connections between social and textual superstructures. At the same time, genres also enable teachers and students to observe how individuals situate themselves in positions of articulation within such superstructures. As such, a genre approach enables us to teach students that writing is more than just a communicative tool, a means of conveying ideas from writer to reader. Writing is not only a skill; it is also a way of being and acting in the world at a particular time, in a particular situation, for the achievement of particular desires. Rather than teaching students some vague and perhaps questionable notion of what "good" writing is, a notion that most likely cannot stand up to disciplinary standards or scrutiny, we gain more by teaching students how to adapt as writers, socially and rhetorically, from one genred site of action to the next. Such repositioning is a critical part of learning to write successfully, as we saw in chapter 5, where students negotiate between the writing prompt and the essay as they learn to write in FYW courses. We ought to promote the idea that good writers adapt well from one genred site of action to the next. The rhetorical art of adaptation or repositioning should become central to our teaching of writing, especially our teaching of invention, which would then become the art of analyzing genres and positioning oneself within them. In what follows, I will describe an approach to writing instruction in FYW that combines genre analysis and invention in such a way as to help student writers begin to access, identify, and participate within genred sites of action.

Genre analysis encourages students to identify and examine the situated desires, subjectivities, relations, and practices that are rhetorically embedded in disciplinary and professional genres. Using genre analysis, we can ask students, for instance, why scientific genres such as lab reports typically use passive sentence constructions, especially when such a rhetorical construction is typically discouraged in humanities, especially in English courses. What does this typified rhetorical feature of the genre reveal about those who use it and their disciplinary (dis)positions, relations, and practices? What position of articulation does the lab report, through the use of this rhetorical feature, maintain for its users? By asking such questions, rather than dismissing outright the passive voice as an undesirable rhetorical strategy or treating it as an arbitrary convention, we locate the passive voice within the discursive and ideological sites of its use—within the scientific genres in which this linguistic construction helps organize and generate scientific practices. Of course, the passive voice alone does not reveal the complex textured sites of scientific activities; to examine these sites, genre analysis, as I will describe momentarily, would need to include identifying a wide array of textual patterns. But early in the course, we can start by making an analysis of the passive voice the occasion for a writing assignment, in which, for instance, we invite students to interview faculty in the sciences, collect samples of lab reports (and other scientific genres), and then analyze and write about what desires, relations, positions, and practices the passive voice generates and organizes in the sciences. In my courses, for example, students have discovered that the passive voice actually serves a crucial disciplinary function in scientific inquiry, reinforcing the scientific imperative that the material world exists objectively, independent of human interaction. They have learned that a scientist assumes the position of one who observes and records what happens, and the passive voice rhetorically enables and reflects this position. Indeed, the passive voice suggests that actions occur largely through their own accord, and the scientist simply describes them. By extracting the actor's role from the action in a sentence such as "Twelve samples were introduced," scientists retain the necessary, even if fictive, objectivity they need to conduct their activities—indeed an objectivity that is critical to a scientist's disciplinary identity. Through their research and our discussions, students learn that the lab report, then, is not merely a means of communicating experimental results; it is also a means by which scientists reproduce and enact scientific subjectivities, desires, and practices—the way they function in the world as scientists. Working as a class, students begin to recognize that the lab report, like any other genre, is a site of action within which users rhetorically acquire, negotiate, and articulate situated desires, subjectivities, and practices. Students in FYW courses can, and I think should, be taught and encouraged to recognize genre as such a site. And they can and should be taught how to use this genre knowledge to develop a rhetorical awareness and agility that will help them navigate disciplinary and professional boundaries as writers long after they leave the FYW course.

In my writing courses, I often begin with a collective genre analysis exercise even before I have explained to students what genre analysis involves. I bring in samples of a genre such as the lab report or the obituary or the greeting card, and I pose the question: what does this kind of text tell us about our culture? In fact, much of what I have learned and describe about the obituary (in chapter 2) and the greeting card (in chapter 4) builds on and adds to these early class discussions. I want students to begin to understand how genre analysis makes sites of activity and the positions of articulation they frame rhetorically visible and accessible to inquiry. Such analysis involves doing a sort of textual archeology, what John Swales has described as "textography" (1998), in which students identify and analyze genres' contexts of use through their rhetorical features. As one FYW student elegantly describes it in the introduction of her genre analysis paper, "the study of genre is not limited to what is clearly seen or presented, such as format, structure, or word choice used in the genre, but extends to the analysis of underlying meanings and social function that can be inferred from the specific features."

In simplest terms, genre analysis involves four steps: collecting samples of the genre, identifying and describing the context of its use, describing its textual patterns, and analyzing what these patterns reveal about the context in which the genre is used. The following heuristic, which I reprint with slight modification from Amy J. Devitt, Anis Bawarshi, and Mary Jo Reiff's *Scenes of Writing: Genre Acts* (in progress), describes these steps.[3]

## Guidelines for Analyzing Genres

1. *Collect Samples of the Genre*

   If you are studying a genre that is fairly public, such as the wedding announcement, you can just look at samples from various newspapers. If you are studying a less public genre, such as the Patient Medical History Form, you might have to visit different doctors' offices to collect samples. If you are unsure where to find samples, ask a user of that genre for assistance. Try to gather samples from more than one place (for example, wedding announcements from different newspapers, medical history forms from different doctors' offices) so that you get a more accurate picture of the complexity of the genre. The more samples of the genre you collect, the more you will be able to notice patterns within the genre.

2. *Study the Situation of the Genre*

   Seek answers to questions such as the ones below.

   *Setting:* Where does the genre appear? Where are texts of this genre typically located? What medium, context? With what other genres does this genre interact?

   *Subject:* What topics is this genre involved with? What issues, ideas, questions, etc. does the genre address? When people use this genre, what is it that they are interacting about?

   *Participants:* Who uses the genre?

   *Writers:* Who writes the texts in this genre? Are multiple writers possible? How do we know who the writers are? What roles do they perform? What characteristics must writers of this genre possess? Under what circumstances do writers write the genre (e.g., in teams, on a computer, in a rush)?

   *Readers:* Who reads the texts in this genre? Is there more than one type of reader for this genre? What roles do they perform? What characteristics must readers of this genre possess? Under what circumstances do readers read the genre (e.g., at their leisure, on the run, in waiting rooms)?

   *Motives:* When is the genre used? For what occasions? Why is the genre used? Why do writers write this genre and why do readers read it? What purposes does the genre fulfill for the people who use it?

3. *Identify and Describe Patterns in the Genre's Features*

What recurrent features do the samples share? For example:

What *content* is typically included? What is excluded? How is the content treated? What sorts of examples are used? What counts as evidence (personal testimony, facts, etc.)?

What *rhetorical appeals* are used? What appeals to logos, pathos, and ethos appear?

How are texts in the genres *structured?* What are their parts, and how are they organized?

In what *format* are texts of this genre presented? What layout or appearance is common? How long is a typical text in this genre?

What types of *sentences* do texts in the genre typically use? How long are they? Are they simple or complex, passive or active? Are the sentences varied? Do they share a certain style?

What *diction* is most common? What types of words are most frequent? Is a type of jargon used? Is slang used? How would you describe the writer's voice?

4. *Analyze What These Patterns Reveal about the Situation*

What do these rhetorical patterns reveal about the genre and the situation in which it is used? Why are these patterns significant? What can you learn about the actions being performed through the genre by observing its language patterns? What arguments can you make about these patterns? As you consider these questions, focus on the following:

What do participants have to *know or believe* to understand or appreciate the genre?

Who is *invited* into the genre, and who is *excluded?*

What *roles* for writers and readers does it encourage or discourage?

What *values, beliefs, goals, and assumptions* are revealed through the genre's patterns?

How is the *subject* of the genre treated? What content is considered most important? What content (topics or details) is ignored?

What *actions* does the genre help make possible? What actions does the genre make difficult?

What *attitude toward readers* is implied in the genre? What attitude toward the world is implied in it?

Notice how the heuristic guides students from the situation to the genre and then back to the situation. First, it asks students to identify the situation from which the genre emerges. Students do this through interviews and observation, trying to identify where and when the genre is used, by whom, and why. After that, students are asked to analyze what the genre tells us about the situation. Such analysis involves describing the genre's rhetorical patterns, from its content down to its diction, and then making an argument about what these patterns reveal about the desires, assumptions, subjectivities, relations, and actions embedded in the genre. In short, students are invited to revisit the situation through the genre that reflects, organizes, and maintains it. As the heuristic suggests, genre analysis enables students and teachers to open a temporary analytical space between the genre and its situation, a space in which students can access and inquire into the interplay between rhetorical and social actions as well as the desires, subjectivities, and relations enacted there. Genre analysis allows teachers to create this analytical space within FYW.

Below are a couple of brief examples of student genre analyses, the first from a FYW course I taught a few years ago and the second from a FYW course I observed last year taught by an advanced graduate student. In the first example, the student elected to study the genres used by nurses in a hospital. After conducting interviews and observing the situations in which the genres are used, the student decided to perform a comparative genre analysis of the screening forms used by registered nurses and nurse practitioners. She examined the different rhetorical patterns of the two genres and then, building on what she had learned from her interviews, analyzed and demonstrated how the genres, in their different rhetorical patterns, reflect, on the one hand, different attitudes about what nurse practitioners and registered nurses do and cannot do, and, on the other, the different positions nurse practitioners and registered nurses occupy within the hospital, including their relation to each other and their patients.

In the second, more recent, example, a student studied the Medical Incident Report that paramedics routinely write after responding to a medical call. Through interviews, the student learned that the report records the time of the call, who responded, the amount of time spent at the scene, as well as pertinent medical information about the patient and the treatment. In addition, the report serves to record the paramedic's performance in the case of potential lawsuits. The student also learned that paramedics dread writing these reports, going so far as to trade the responsibility for chores. After moving from the situation to the text, the student then returned to the situation through the text. She described and analyzed the report's features, including its use of trauma codes and abbreviations, its compact textual spaces for recording information, and its short and terse sentences. These features, she argues, invite an impersonal, seemingly unbiased description of the event. Remarkably, the student concludes that the presence of this genre reminds the paramedics of what is expected of them. It is one of several genres that frame how paramedics experience their work. The student describes this intertextuality as follows:

> When the call goes out, the firefighter and paramedics receive the minimum amount of information over the scanner. On the way to the scene, the paramedics are already formulating what they may find, based on what they heard over the scanner. This "seeing" comes from words. Once on the scene . . . the [paramedic] must either continue with the preexisting plan, or throw it out based on what they can see. When writing the [report], the paramedics know that they are doing so in order that others not present at the incident will be able to "see" what happened and therefore make judgments on the patient's behavior, treatment, and how well the paramedics responded.

Through genre analysis, the student in this case has used the genre of the Medical Incident Report to gain access into the complex, multitextured world of paramedics, and to describe how this textured world frames the way paramedics see and are seen.

Once students and I establish that genres can tell us things about those who use them, and after students have had a chance to analyze a genre of their choosing, I have then instructed students to form semester-long groups, each adopting a specific academic discipline (for example, an economics group, a chemistry group, a psychology group, and so on). Working in groups, students study the discipline through its genres. They interview faculty and students in the discipline to find out what sorts of texts they write and what function writing serves. They then collect sample genres from the discipline, and, working individually, each student analyzes one of the genres following procedures I have described above. Based on that analysis, students then establish a claim about what the genre reveals and then write an argument essay that presents and develops that claim with evidence from the analysis.[4]

Genre analysis gives rhetoric a central focus in FYW courses. Rather than having students write about topics such as race, gender, gay rights, the environment, animal rights, flag burning, the death penalty, the media, and so on (important topics all), we can encourage students instead to write about how different genres position writers to write about these topics—to write, that is, about writing: how genres affect writers' rhetorical choices, what genred desires might be motivating these rhetorical choices, what attitudes are embedded in writers' rhetorical choices, how rhetorical choices affect meaning, and so on. Students still write arguments, but these arguments are about writing, about the rhetorical choices writers make and how their genred positions of articulation organize and elicit these choices. Indeed, which genre my students choose to study is not as relevant as what they learn about invention by analyzing and writing about it. Invention, as I have defined it, takes place within and grows out of such a rhetorical awareness. We can make the teaching of invention a great deal less mysterious if we base it in a process of genre analysis that allows students to inquire into and position themselves within the discursive and ideological frameworks of genres. This is how I propose we teach invention in FYW courses.

Through genre analysis, we can teach FYW students to recognize how rhetorical habits are dynamically connected to disciplinary habitats.[5] As advocates of WID argue, this recognition should go a long way in dispelling some of the guesswork and mystery that students so often experience while writing. In my classes, students learn that when they write in a certain genre, they are participating in a textured site of action, which means they are engaging in certain desires which underwrite certain commitments, subjectivities, relations, and practices. If they are able to begin identifying what these desires are—that is, if they are able to analyze how these desires are rhetorically constituted—then they will be able to invent themselves and participate in the genred sites of action more meaningfully and critically as writers, as we saw in the examples of the social work student learning to write an assessment report in chapter 4, and the FYW students navigating between the textured worlds of the writing prompt and student essay in chapter 5. An explicit knowledge of genres can lead students to make more effective rhetorical decisions because they will have a better sense of what purposes their rhetorical choices are serving. That is, rather than guessing, they will be more likely to predict the effects of their rhetorical strategies, including the position they will need to assume in order to produce these strategies. Through genre analysis, then, we not only make students aware of different rhetorical conventions and what they reveal, but we also make students aware of how these different conventions position them as writers, the kinds of positions they need to assume as they reproduce these conventions. Such analysis allows students, to borrow a phrase from Victor Villanueva, to achieve a kind of critical cultural literacy (1993) in which they learn the rules of the genre game and participate in it at the same time. This can be empowering for students.

Because writing is not only a communicative but also a social act, involving communicants in social relations and actions, it necessarily involves a process of repositioning. Individuals, for example, become social workers, patients, and students in part by learning how to position themselves rhetorically within such genres as the assessment report, the PMHF, and the syllabus. Invention is the process through which writers locate themselves within these genred positions of articulation. Invention and repositioning go hand in hand. For this reason, some critics of the explicit teaching of genre argue that it is impossible to study and teach genres outside of their disciplinary habitats, since to write genres effectively requires not just formal knowledge of their rhetorical features but also social knowledge of their disciplinary assumptions (see Giltrow and Valiquette 1994). In addition, they argue, since we learn to write genres tacitly as part of being and acting in a certain discipline, teachers cannot expect students to learn genres in the artificial context of the classroom (see Freedman 1993a; 1993b). Certainly, as FYW teachers we cannot possibly initiate our students into the various disciplinary genres of the university, let alone the various professional genres they will encounter outside the university. We have neither the time nor the expertise to do so. What we can do, however, is teach our students how to become more rhetorically astute and agile, how, in other words, to use genre analysis as a way to become more effective and critical "readers" of the sites of action within which writing takes place. Such an analytical skill *is* transferable and does not require immersion in disciplinary cultures. In many ways, it is a skill our students already possess, since to survive as social beings we must all possess at least a modicum of rhetorical awareness. When they enter a room, especially an unfamiliar room, for example, most students first survey or "scope out" the scene. They first analyze who is in the room, how different people are dressed, how the room is structured, who is talking to whom, in what way, on what subject, and so on. Such an analysis of the scene enables them to position themselves and participate within it more effectively. Students are already rhetorically perceptive and adjust at times with uncanny ease from one discursive and ideological context to the next—from their dorm lives to their classroom lives to their family lives and so on. As teachers of writing, we can build upon these skills by teaching students that genre analysis (the process of "reading" a site of action as it is rhetorically embedded in its genres), invention (the process of positioning oneself within these genred sites), and social activities (the choices a writer makes and their effects within these genred sites) are connected in the act of writing.

Unfortunately, most students have not been taught to understand writing as "one of the activities by which we locate ourselves in the enmeshed systems that make up the social world" (Cooper and Holzman 1989, 13). They do not see writing, particularly academic writing, as being as socially embedded as the rest of their discursive lives, and so do not bring their rich social and rhetorical skills to bear on their writing. This is due in part, I think, to the way that invention continues to be taught largely as a private act in many FYW courses. However, if we can teach students to recognize and write about how "the enmeshed systems that make up the social world" are rhetorically embedded within genres—if, that is, we can help students recognize that genres are very much like rhetorical and social spaces (or topoi) they locate themselves and participate within—then we can go a long way towards helping students more effectively and critically to invent themselves and participate as writers within the various disciplinary scenes of the university. Such a recognition grounds writing instruction not only in the processes of textual production, but also in what texts do in the world—their function and effects. This kind of rhetorical approach teaches students how to write by first teaching them how to place themselves within the different enmeshed systems that are reflected and maintained textually in different genres.

At the same time as it helps connect FYW and WID, a genre-based writing pedagogy also justifies the place of FYW in English. We do not need to be social workers or scientists or doctors to know how to inquire into assessment reports, lab reports, or Patient Medical History Forms. As scholars and teachers of English, we are, more than anything else, experts in language use: what language does, how it does it, to what ends, where, when, and why. As a result, we are uniquely qualified to teach students how to inquire into various disciplinary and professional genres, in some ways perhaps even more so than those who use them on a daily basis (see C. Miller 1999; Maimon 1983). As Richard Coe has written, "genres embody attitudes," but since "those attitudes are built into generic structures, they are sometimes danced without conscious awareness or intent on the part of the individual using the genre" (1994a, 183). By moving a genre from its context of use to the analytical space of the FYW course, genre analysis enables teachers and students to temporarily make conscious, scrutinize, and practice the unconscious attitudes that are embedded within genres.

My goal in using genre analysis in FYW is not the acquisition of disciplinary knowledge per se. My goal, rather, is to encourage students to understand invention as rhetorically grounded, so that invention involves a process in which writers (re)position themselves and participate within discursive and ideological formations.[6] In short, I use genre analysis as an invention technique, a heuristic which does not so much ask students to imagine themselves as the starting point of writing as it encourages them to write by inquiring into and then situating themselves within genred positions of articulation. As situated topoi, genres thus serve as the loci of invention, the habits as well as the habitats for acting in language. In fact, I am continuously surprised at how astute students are in recognizing the positions of articulation embedded in the genres they study. One student, whom I cited in chapter 4, revealed how the PMHF constructs the patient as an embodied object; others analyzed how wedding invitations rhetorically position the bride as property, how different genres within a hospital locate registered nurses and nurse practitioners into different positions, how different grade reporting genres (from traditional report cards to the more recent grade continuums) position students as different kinds of learners, and so on. Most importantly, students recognize how these positions are constructed rhetorically within the genres they study. They may never become doctors or social workers or teachers or brides, but they have learned something valuable, I think, about how writing works to make these positions possible. This knowledge can travel with them to any genred space they encounter. I consider such knowledge of genre as central to a knowledge of invention, the first step in helping writers learn how to position themselves and participate meaningfully and critically within different genred sites of action.

Once students are done practicing genre analysis, I have at times asked them to write some of these genres, thereby moving from analysis to production of texts. Again, I confess I am less concerned with what genres students write, and more concerned with how they rationalize their rhetorical choices when they write these genres. For this reason, I require students to submit a rationale along with their written genres. In this rationale, students essentially make an argument on behalf of their rhetorical choices as these are informed by what they have come to know about the desires, subjectivities, relations, and practices embedded in the genre. This rationale becomes especially significant in those cases where students choose to resist and or transform a genre based on what they have learned about it. In such cases, students can explain which genre features they have chosen to resist and why, thereby speculating on the effects and consequences of their changes. This sort of metarhetorical skill can help students navigate what Lovitt and Young have described as "the rhetorical and social realities of either academic or nonacademic writing" (1997, 116). Indeed, this is the sort of skill that I think Frances Christie refers to when she writes, "Learning the genres of one's culture is both part of entering into it with understanding, and part of developing the necessary ability to change it" (1988, 30). Such a metarhetorical awareness of genre can serve students beyond the FYW course and into the various writing situations they will encounter in the university and beyond.

There persists a frustrating assumption that FYW is a content-less course, that it has no inherent subject. In this chapter, I have tried to demonstrate that FYW *does* have a subject; it is writing.

Writing is the subject of FYW. Not just the process of writing, but writing itself—what writing does, how it works, and why—should be the subject of FYW. In other words, FYW should become a course in rhetoric, a course that uses genres to teach students how to recognize and navigate discursive and ideological formations. We can do more to help our students write in and beyond the disciplines by teaching them how to position themselves rhetorically within genres so that they can more effectively meet (and potentially change) the desires and practices embedded there. Such a pedagogy challenges us to locate invention at the intersection between the acquisition and articulation of desire where writers and writing take place. By locating the FYW course at this nexus, we stand a better chance of justifying both the course's relationship to WID and its very existence within the English department and the university.

## CONCLUSION

Since beginnings are continuations, the end of this book is destined to become the beginning of another. So in that spirit, let me conclude by returning to the subject of beginnings with which this book began. In *Heart of Darkness*, Joseph Conrad describes what amounts to be such a return, a journey toward beginnings—the *heart* of darkness. The narrator, Marlow, describes his journey up the Congo in this way: "Going up that river was like traveling back to the earliest *beginnings* of the world, when vegetation rioted on the earth and the big trees were kings" (1988, 35; my emphasis). In some ways, this is a colonialist fantasy that imagines the colonized space as site of origin for the colonizers' self-(re)production. But beginnings are a problem in this novel. First is the question of where or when the story begins. Does it begin on board the *Nellie*, the moored sailing vessel on which Marlow begins his narrative? Or does it begin earlier, with the frame-narrator's narrative of Marlow's narrative? Better yet, does the story begin even earlier than that, prior to the *Nellie* and the frame- narrator, with Marlow's fictitious experiences in the Congo? Or does it begin earlier even, in

Conrad's "Congo Diary," which he kept while he served as a captain of a steamboat on the Congo? Or does it begin with the colonialism that brought Conrad to the Congo in the first place and shaped his experiences there? These questions suggest the extent to which beginnings always take place in relation to other beginnings—in the midst of other beginnings.

*Heart of Darkness* does not only problematize its own beginnings, however; it also questions the very nature of beginnings as unpreceded origins, as what Edward Said terms "divine" beginnings. Marlow journeys up the Congo in search of Kurtz, who signifies an essence of something buried deep in the "heart" of darkness. Marlow's is a search for beginnings, for what Derrida calls a "transcendental signified" (1992, 1118) represented by Kurtz. But what Marlow actually discovers when he finally locates Kurtz is that such a transcendent, unified, self-generated beginning does not exist. What he realizes instead is that Kurtz is a sign or "word," so that the scene of beginnings becomes a scene of interpretation. Beginnings exist as moments of interpretation, not origination, just like signs only mean as they are interpreted. Kurtz only means as Marlow interprets him, so that each beginning is an interpretation and a continuation of another beginning, a series of secular, dialogical beginnings functioning in relation to one another in much the same way that Bakhtin describes utterances as "filled with echoes and reverberations of other utterances" (1986, 91).

In the same way, I have argued that writers and writing begin in relation to genres, the discursive and ideological conditions that writers have to position themselves within and interpret in order to write. By encouraging student writers to recognize beginnings as genred positions of articulation, and by teaching students how to inquire into these positions, we enable them to locate themselves more critically and effectively as writers within these beginnings. That is, we teach them how to begin their own writing in relation to these already existing beginnings.

# NOTES

NOTES TO CHAPTER ONE

1.  Composition textbooks such as Bazerman's *Involved*, Hatch's *Arguing in Communities*, Klooster and Bloem's *The Writer's Community*, and Trimbur's *Call to Write*, to name a few, increasingly acknowledge and present writing and invention as thoroughly situational and cooperative activities. Trimbur's book, in particular, applies current theories of genre to teach students how to write different texts, and has enjoyed some success. And an increasing number of textbooks use ethnographic techniques to teach students how to identify and examine scenes of writing.

2.  For a more detailed account of the conditions that helped construct this view of the autonomous author, including the role of the printing press and the emergence of copyright law, which designated the text as the property of its author, see M. Rose 1993 and Woodmansee and Jaszi 1994.

NOTES TO CHAPTER TWO

1.  In describing genres as sites of action, we must acknowledge that genres do not only help us make certain activities happen; they also help prevent other activities from happening. As such, genres function as sites of articulation and silence. What cannot be articulated is as significant as what can be, and any theorization of genre needs to account for the power and politics of genre. For more on the relation between genre and the politics of articulation, see Paré (2002) and Schryer (2002).

2.  In literary studies, scholarship in cultural studies is a notable and more recent exception. Scholars in cultural studies recognize and treat all texts, literary or otherwise, as cultural artifacts, which reflect and reproduce cultural contexts and

everyday social practices. For cultural studies work that examines theories of the everyday, see Michel de Certeau's *The Practice of Everyday Life* (1984).

3.  As I am describing it, the genre function is akin to what Pierre Bourdieu calls *habitus*, which he defines in *The Logic of Practice* as "the system of structured, structuring dispositions" (1990, 52) and in *Practical Reason* as a kind of "practical sense for what is to be done in a given situation—what is called in sport a 'feel' for the game, that is, the art of anticipating the future of the game, which is inscribed in the present state of play" (1998, 25). As Bourdieu is careful to note, the habitus is not only a symbolic structure, but is rather "constituted in practice and is always oriented towards practical functions" (1990, 52).

4.  For those who, like Benedetto Croce (1968) and Maurice Blanchot (1959), perceive literary texts as being indeterminate, an expression of unbounded imagination, genre is an institutional threat to literary texts and authors. Echoing in part the formalist and new critical dream of a free-standing text made up of its own internal relations and subject to its own structural integrity, Blanchot perceives genre as a threat to the text's autonomy. He writes: "The book alone is important, as it is, far from genre, outside rubrics . . . under which it refuses to be arranged and to which it denies the power to fix its place and to determine its form" (qtd. in Perloff 1989). Even poststructuralist critiques of formalism subordinate genres. Questioning the stability of structures and exposing the contradictions and fissures within what appears to be a self-contained and coherent text, poststructuralist theorists have highlighted the instability and arbitrariness of meaning. In relation to such textual indeterminacy, genre exists tenuously. For example, Jacques Derrida, who in his "Law of Genre" acknowledges that "every text participates in one or several genres; there is no genre-less text" (1980, 65), insists that the "law" of genre, as with any other kind of law, is an arbitrary and conservative attempt to impose order on what is ultimately indeterminate.

Even scholars such as Cohen (1989), Hirsch (1967), Perloff (1989), and Rosmarin (1985) who recognize the heuristic function of genre nonetheless subordinate it to an *ad hoc* status, one that not only classifies but also explains texts. These critics are careful to note, however, that even though genre may exercise some explanatory power over literary texts, it does not interfere with their autonomy. Literary texts are produced and exist independently of genres; genres function only as critical apparatuses. Genre is, therefore, the critic's tool or heuristic, a lens the critic uses to interpret literary texts. The same text can be subject to different genre-lenses without compromising its imagined integrity.

5.    Carolyn Miller takes up this idea of genre as chronotope when she explains, "genres impose structure on a given action in space-time" (1994a, 75). For more on genre and the way it shapes and regulates space-time, see Bakhtin (1981), Bazerman (1994b), Schryer (2002), and Yates and Orlikowski (2002). Of course, the idea that genres constitute certain space-time configurations is not as recent or novel as it may seem. The classical triad of lyric, epic, and dramatic, which can be traced back to Plato and Aristotle and which Genette calls "archigenres," has received considerable attention in literary studies (see, for example, Frye 1957; Genette 1992; Scholes 1975; Welleck and Warren 1942). The triad has served as the basis for a great deal of literary generic categorizations, and has often been associated with space-time configurations, especially with spatial presence and temporal perspective. Lyric, for instance, is often defined as subjective, dramatic as objective, and epic as subjective-objective (Genette 1992, 38), so that in each formation we have a different notion of presence—each, that is, articulates a different spatial dimension in which action takes place. Within lyric, the writer exists in spatial proximity to his or her text, being in the text, so to speak, whereas in the dramatic, the action takes place in its own spatial context that determines the interaction between two independent actors. Spatially, we equate objectivity with distance and subjectivity with proximity and intimacy. Temporally, lyric is often associated with the present, dramatic with the future, and epic with the past (Genette 1992, 47-49), so that each archigenre represents a particular

way of conceiving of literary temporality that, needless to say, will affect literary actions within that temporality. So the lyric, dramatic, and epic archigenres orient the way that time, space, and the activities that occur within them are configured and enacted in different literary texts.

6.    This is particularly the case for scholars working in cultural studies. Stephen Greenblatt, for example, introduces the special issue of the journal *Genre* dealing with the power of form in the construction of Renaissance culture by claiming that "the study of genre is an exploration of the poetics of culture" (1982, 6). Similarly, Terry Threadgold argues that genre "cannot be treated in isolation from the social realities and processes which it contributes to maintaining (and could be used to subvert)" (1989, 103).

7.    For a more comprehensive discussion of the difficulties associated with the concept of discourse community and how scholars in genre theory respond to these difficulties, see Bawarshi, Devitt, and Reiff's "Materiality and Genre in the Study of Discourse Community."

8.    Thomas O. Beebee, defining genre as the "use-value" of texts, in part applies what Bakhtin claims for speech genres to written genres. For Beebee, "primarily, genre is the precondition for the creation and the reading of texts" (1994, 250), because genre provides the ideological context in which a text and its participants function and attain cultural value: "Genre gives us not understanding in the abstract and passive sense but use in the pragmatic and active sense" (14). The kind of use-value a genre represents depends on who its users are, on what practices it makes possible, and on its relation to other genres within a sphere of speech communication. It is within this social and rhetorical economy that a genre attains its use-value, making genre one of the bearers, articulators, and reproducers of culture—in short, ideological. In turn, genres are what make texts ideological, endowing them with a social use-value. As ideological-discursive formations, then, genres delimit all language—not just poetic language—into what Beebee calls the "possibilities of its usage."

9. In raising genre to the level of register, I follow J.R. Martin (1992, 1997) who defines genres as textured relations of field, mode, and tenor. In so doing, I do not mean to suggest that genre constitutes or accounts for the entire social sphere that we call culture, or, for that matter, that genre accounts for the social sphere of the university or even a classroom within the university. Each of these social spheres, in addition to other social and material forces at work within them, contains multiple, sometimes competing genres that, grouped together, allow us to map these spheres rhetorically. Indeed, the genre function itself is a function of these larger social spheres, at once reflecting, reproducing, and potentially transforming them. By claiming that genres function as registers, then, I am only referring to the ways in which genres maintain and articulate specific relations of field, tenor, and mode within these social spheres.

10. Others working in genre studies have also considered the impact of Giddens's theory of structuration on theories of genre. Carol Berkenkotter and Thomas Huckin were among the first to do so in their "Rethinking Genre From a Sociocognitive Perspective" (1993), positing that genre is both constitutive of social structure and generative of social practice (495). See also Yates and Orlikowski (1992) and Giltrow and Valiquette (1994).

11. Not all scholars working in rhetorical genre studies are willing to make such a claim for genre. For instance, John Swales, whose *Genre Analysis* has contributed so much to rhetorical genre studies, locates genre as one of six characteristics shared by members of a discourse community in order to achieve their goals. As Swales puts it, "genres are communicative vehicles for the achievement of goals" (1990, 46). Yet Swales overlooks what his own analysis seems to reveal: the functional as well as epistemological nature of genres. For example, he concludes that the research article (RA) is a "quite different genre to the laboratory report and has its own quite separate conventions, its own processes of literary reasoning and its own standards of arguments" (1990, 118-19).

He then delineates these conventions in order to teach students how to write RAs. Yet he does not consider or explain what these differences reveal about the way each genre sets up its own social and rhetorical representation of science or, for that matter, how the different processes of reasoning that each genre allows affect how its writers recognize and experience their subject matter or themselves as subjects. All we are left with is Swales' suggestive claim that the RA is a "remarkable phenomenon, so cunningly engineered by rhetorical machining that it somehow still gives an impression of being but a simple description of relatively untransmitted raw material" (1990, 125). We are left to wonder about how the RA actually represents a particular space-time configuration of laboratory practice as well as about how the "impression" that the genre creates actually shapes its users' versions of laboratory practice in certain RA-mediated ways.

## NOTES TO CHAPTER THREE

1. As Rebecca Moore Howard points out, autonomy and agency are not synonymous: "The issue of autonomy is an issue of whether the writer acts alone, whereas the issue of agency is one of whether the writer acts or is in action" (1999, 46). Following Howard, I do not think we deny the agency of the writer by denying its autonomy.

2. It is tempting to think about "freewriting" as a genre that denies its status and function as a genre, a free and unmediated space for the exploration of ideas. Perceived as such, freewriting might be understood as a genre that invites its users to fantasize about its non-existence, which only makes it a more extreme case of the fantasy that all genres desire their users to maintain. As Edward Said suggests, "In a human life . . . it might appear possible to believe in the freedom of one's initiative or of one's action; at the same time, when such freedom is viewed from a more accurate perspective, the same activity is seen to be unfree" (1975, 133).

3. Even more recent incarnations of process theory, which problematize the notion of the writer as stable and coherent,

still define writing in terms of its writer. For example, in her "Places to Stand: The Reflective Writer-Teacher-Writer in Composition" (1999), Wendy Bishop describes the role of what she calls the writer who teaches and the teacher who writes. Implicit in her definitions of "writer" and "writing" throughout the essay is a focus on the figure of the writer present in the writing. According to Bishop, teachers who write are distinguished by their interest "in the act of writing from a writer's perspective" (1999, 14).

4. This modern epistemology, based in empiricism, was heavily influenced by John Locke. In his *Essay Concerning Human Understanding*, published in 1690, Locke argued that individuals, born with no innate ideas, gain knowledge through accumulated experiences. Through sensory impressions, the mind stores simple ideas and then, with the help of the understanding or reason, associates and categorizes them into more complex, abstract ideas. If the logical faculties of the mind are functioning accurately—that is, if there is no interference from such "illogical" faculties as the emotions or imagination—then an individual's accumulated knowledge and understanding of the world should reflect and be confirmed by other individuals' knowledge and understanding. Because words are how individuals label and communicate ideas, Locke fears rhetoric's influence. Rhetoric, what Locke calls "that powerful instrument of error and deceit" (1992, 268), is a threat to such an empirical epistemology, for "if we would speak of things as they are, we must allow that all the art of rhetoric, *besides order and clearness*, all the artificial and figurative application of words eloquence hath invented, are for nothing else but to insinuate wrong ideas, move the passions, and thereby mislead the judgment, and so indeed are perfect cheats" (Locke 268; my emphasis). In Locke's formulation of rhetoric, a formulation that was to influence later eighteenth and nineteenth century views of rhetorical invention, rhetoric was no longer a generative art but a regulative skill involving order and clearness.

5. In his now classic definition, Richard Young describes some key characteristics of current-traditional rhetoric: "The emphasis

on the composed product rather than the composing process; the analysis of discourse in words, sentences, and paragraphs; the classification of discourse into description, narration, exposition, and argument; the strong concern with usage (syntax, spelling, punctuation) and with style (economy, clarity, emphasis); the preoccupation with the informal essay and the research paper; and so on" (1978, 31). Sharon Crowley adds: "Current-traditional rhetoric occults the mentalism that underlies its introspective theory of invention," assuming that ideas and subjects exist prior to their representation in discourse, which becomes a graphic embodiment of the invention process (1990, 13). For an overview of current-traditional rhetoric and its impact on the teaching of writing, see James Berlin (1987), Sharon Crowley (1990), and Robert Connors (1997).

6.    Of course, it was well before the 1950s that scholars began exploring the cognitive *and* creative workings of the mind. By 1790, for instance, Immanuel Kant was arguing that we are born with apriori cognitive categories which help us conceptualize what we experience through our sense impressions, so that our understanding is not necessarily a reflection of the natural world as Descartes had assumed. In addition, only twenty years after Locke published his *Essay*, Joseph Addison was already wondering if the imagination was indeed as dangerous and distorting as Locke had suggested. While he acknowledges, following Locke, that our ideas are derived from external impressions imposed on our senses, he also suggests that we gain a great deal of pleasure when our minds extend and transform these impressions through the imagination. In so doing, Addison endowed the imagination with a creative power. So did Edward Young, who, in *Conjectures on Original Composition* (1759), presages the romantic movement by arguing that some individuals are endowed with innate genius that allows them not only to imitate but also to originate (1992, 332-33). To counter the passivity of imitation, Young concludes by advising individuals (in terms strikingly similar to those Rohman uses a little more than two hundred years later) to "therefore dive deep into thy bosom; learn the

depth, extent, bias, and full forte of thy mind; contract full intimacy with the stranger within thee" (336).

7.   Recent work in creativity theory also acknowledges such formations. For instance, Mihaly Csikszentmihalyi and his colleagues have described what they call the Domain Individual Field Interaction (DIFI) model to offset the tendency in creativity research to locate creativity in a person (Feldman et al 1994, 24). In order to function creatively within a field, an individual must be familiar with its organized body of knowledge or domain, including its "representational techniques," "symbol systems," "special terms," and "technologies" (Feldman et al., 22). The "locus of creativity," Csikszentmihalyi claims, is the dynamic interaction between the domain, the individual, and the field (Feldman et al., 21). For other examples, see Kuhn (1970), Beaugrande (1979), and Weisberg (1993).

8.   In describing genres as situated topoi, I am expanding the classical definition of topoi not only to include general sets of questions through which a rhetor can explore any given subject (topoi as analytical tools) but also, as the name suggests, to include locales within which such exploration takes place. By comparing genres to topoi, I am suggesting that genres represent situated sites of inquiry and action, habits as well as habitats for recognizing, exploring, and enacting arguments, situations, and identities. I do not intend the comparison to be literal, only to suggest that, like the topoi, genres are situated social and rhetorical sites in which invention takes place.

## NOTES TO CHAPTER FOUR

1.   My main concern in this and the following chapter is to describe and analyze how genres shape and enable writers as social actors who rhetorically enact certain subjectivities, relations, and practices as they write. The question of degree, of how much genres influence writers, may be impossible to quantify. As we will shortly see, genres, both conceptually and textually, maintain social conventions for how we recognize and act in various situations. How much we as social actors are influenced by these conventions depends on factors such

as our past experiences (especially with other genres); our social positioning, including our gender, class, race, and ethnicity; our immediate circumstances; and other psychological and biological X-factors. All these factors shape how we interpret generic conventions, but the fact of these conventions remains as a necessary condition within and against which we enact our intentions and subjectivities.

2. What becomes apparent in such places as Florida is that even those contexts that seem outside of our rhetorical range are nonetheless rhetorically bounded. The difference between so-called "wild" and "not-wild" environments is as much rhetorical as it is geographical. We recognize a place as wild mainly because we designate it as such, and we act in such a place according to accepted social norms. These norms are rhetorically rehearsed for us in such places as National Parks' visitors centers which not only narrate the nature of the wilderness we are about to enter—and how, subsequently, we should behave in this environment—but also place us conceptually within this narrative/environment. In short, even in places that seem outside of rhetoric, places we call "wilderness" or "nature," we cannot escape the power of rhetoric in shaping how we socially define, recognize, and experience our environments and ourselves in relation to them.

3. I am indebted to Teresa Tran, a pre-med student enrolled in a genre-based writing course I taught in the Spring of 1997 at the University of Kansas, for prompting my interest in the patient medical history form and for her insights into how such forms reflect and support medical assumptions. For related work in doctor patient interaction and subject formation, see Berkenkotter (2001).

4. The sketchbooks serve a similar function to what Janet Giltrow calls a "meta-genre," which she defines as an "atmosphere of wordings and activities, demonstrated precedents or sequestered expectations—atmospheres surrounding genres" (2002, 195). But in addition to being atmospheres, the sketchbooks are themselves genres, so it might be more accurate to call them alpha genres instead.

5.  As I take Giddens to mean, and as I conceive of it, reproduction is not the same as duplication. When we reproduce something, we are not producing an exact copy of it because any reproduction necessarily involves some variation. This is the case biologically, linguistically, and rhetorically. For instance, biological ecosystems are not static because they change as the organisims living within them reproduce and evolve. The same is true for genres. In helping reproduce rhetorical environments, genres also help communicants change rhetorical environments because on some level writing genres always involves some interpretation, which involves some variation.

6.  As an example of how unique circumstances can over-ride situational motives, we can imagine that the patient who writes the allegory may be friends with the physician, and so the physician will recognize the allegory as more of a friendly, playful gesture, a way of signaling intimacy, rather than an act of resistance. But the effect of this genre transgression nonetheless remains a function of the genre.

7.  For a related example, see Thomas Pfau's study of lyric poetry and authorship, "The Pragmatics of Genre: Moral Theory and Lyric Authority in Hegel and Wordsworth," in which he argues that lyric poetry is not, as popularly assumed, merely a vehicle for expressing private consciousness. For example, Wordsworth's "Ode to Duty," Pfau argues, "does not 'express' a newly discovered spiritual conviction but, instead, realigns (and thereby empowers as a cultural 'authority') the self with a historically proven social value, here present as an 'iterable' genre" (1994,154-5).

8.  Anthony Paré (2002) provides a good example of how genres can create tensions that might lead to resistance and transformation. He describes the struggles northern Canadian Inuit social workers encounter as they use social work genres developed in southern, urban Canada. This use forced the Inuit workers "into a position between cultures and into the role of professional representatives of the colonial power" (63). Genres naturalize desires and ideologies, making the actions they elicit seem common sensible, but when these desires

and ideologies encounter conflicting desires and ideologies, their illusion of common sense is fractured. This tension, however, does not necessarily lead to genre change in part because southern, urban social work genres represent dominant ideologies and desires. For examples of how genres change over time because of changes in technology, ideology, and context, see Bazerman (1988), Freedman and Smart (1997), and Popken (1999).

9.  Of course, there are some positions that Michael cannot occupy without obtaining a certain social status, even if he had access to the appropriate genres. For example, he would not "become" a doctor simply because he knew how to write a prescription note, and he would not become a lawyer simply because he knew how to write a legal brief. There are roles we earn through education, election, and practice (all of which certainly involve a range of genres) that work in conjunction with the subject positions we occupy. Genres and roles are mixed in with one another, so that, for instance, a judge is someone who is shaped and enabled by both her status and her genres. Both necessarily interact.

10. I should note here that sub-genres are not the same as textual variations within a genre. Such variations are a mark of all genres. More accurately, sub-genres are typified variations within a genre that nonetheless still share significant social and rhetorical motives with that genre. Sub-genres typify their own more specific situations within the larger socio-rhetorical situations of the genre. John Swales refers to the various sub-genres that constitute a genre such as the GC as "multi-genres" (1990, 38-61).

NOTES TO CHAPTER FIVE

1.  It is worth noting here that the word "ethos" in Greek means "a habitual gathering place" (Campbell 1989, 122). Just like rhetorical strategy, then, the persona a rhetor assumes takes place within a place, a habitation or topoi, so that when rhetors invent, they are not only formulating the available means of persuasion, but also the rhetorical persona they

need to carry out that rhetorical strategy. As LeFevre explains, "ethos . . . appears in that socially created space, in the 'between,' the point of intersection between speaker or writer and listener or reader" (1987, 46). Considered as situated topoi, genres not only shape and enable how communicants recognize and enact social situations; genres also shape and enable how communicants recognize and enact their ethos or subjectivities within these situations.

2.   With the increased use of computer technology in education, especially networked classes and distance learning, this claim becomes less generalizable. If anything, though, the emergence of the "virtual classroom" only strengthens my claims about genre and the classroom that follow.

3.   It is worth noting that the FYW classroom is no more artificial than Epcot is "artificial" when compared to the "real" Florida. As I discussed in chapter 4, Epcot is as complex a rhetorical ecosystem as any wilderness-designated area. Both are rhetorical constructions, ways we define, conceptualize, and behave in our environments.

4.   For this analysis, I randomly collected fifteen syllabi from colleagues at a research university and from published teaching guides. All the syllabi are from FYW courses, and reflect a balance between experienced and new teachers.

5.   The examples I analyze in this section are culled from my examination of fifteen randomly collected writing prompts from experienced and new teachers of FYW at a research university.

6.   I reprint this and the following student excerpts as they appear in the students' essays, errors and all.

NOTES ON CHAPTER SIX

1.   Certainly, a great deal has happened to mark the return of rhetoric since the FYW course was first developed at Harvard in 1874. Fred Newton Scott at the University of Michigan fought and was successful for years during the early part of the twentieth century in maintaining a program in rhetoric, producing some of the country's only Ph.Ds in rhetoric. And the 1960s witnessed what James Berlin (1987) and others have

referred to as a renaissance of rhetoric—what Ken Macrorie, then editor of *College Composition and Communication,* dubbed the "new rhetoric" in 1964. In fact, at the 1963 Conference on College Composition and Communication, the "Rhetoric in Freshman English" workshop, led in part by Wayne Booth, Virginia Burke, Francis Christensen, Edward P.J. Corbett, and Richard Young, passed the following two resolutions: "Resolved, that rhetoric, generally conceived as effective adaptation of writing skills to particular ends and/or audiences, be accepted as an integral part of the freshman course" and "Rhetorical principles should be the organizational principle of the freshman English course and the evaluating criteria for grading student papers" (qtd. in Connors 1997, 206). Yet, while the rhetorical turn has had a significant effect on the increased interest in rhetorical theory in literary and nonliterary studies as well as the sciences over the last forty or so years, and while it has played a major role in helping establish composition studies as an academic, not just a teaching, subject, it did not have as great an impact on writing instruction. As David Fleming has recently argued, the revival of rhetoric remains a scholarly phenomenon, one marked by "relative failure at the level of undergraduate education" (1998, 169).

2.    I am aware of what post-structuralist theories have taught us, that we cannot escape structure even when we try to observe or even critique structure. There is no structure-free stance, and I do not presume such a stance for FYW. I do argue, however, that its position within English departments (which share, if anything, a focus on critical language study) affords the course the kind of rhetorical vantage that can position it within a structure while allowing it to observe what Derrida has called the structurality of that structure (1992).

3.    Amy J. Devitt, Mary Jo Reiff, and I describe and develop these steps in much greater detail in a composition textbook we are currently completing tentatively called *Scenes of Writing: Genre Acts* (forthcoming, Longman), a book that teaches students to read and write their way into different scenes of writing—academic, public, and workplace—through their genres.

4. Before students write their argument essays, I lead the class in a collective genre analysis of the argument essay, in which we use the guidelines for analyzing genres to identify and interrogate the goals, values, and assumptions embedded in this FYW genre and the position it invites them to assume in relation to the subject matter. This allows the students and me to examine what it means to make academic arguments.

5. For more arguments on behalf of the explicit teaching of genre in writing courses, which involves exposing the formal and rhetorical features of genres and articulating their underlying social motives and assumptions, see, for example, Christie (1988); Fahnestock (1993); Lovitt and Young (1997); Maimon (1983); and Williams and Colomb (1993).

6. I want to emphasize here that my pedagogy does not aim for assimilation into genred sites of action; it aims, rather, for a critical understanding and participation. I have discovered that as students begin to uncover the desires, subjectivities, and activities embedded in a genre's rhetorical conventions, they not only develop the ability to reproduce the genre more effectively; they also develop the desire to change it. Teresa Tran, for example, who studied the PMHF in my course, recognized something empowering in genre analysis when she used it to uncover how doctors rhetorically and materially treat patients as embodied objects. She insisted that when she became a doctor, she would lobby the American Medical Association to change the PMHF under the assumption that a change in the genre's rhetorical features would result in a change in the social practices these feature make possible. Indeed, genre literacy and critical literacy go hand-in-hand.

# REFERENCES

Adams, Hazard, Ed. 1992. *Critical Theory Since Plato*. Rev. ed. Fort Worth: Harcourt Brace Jovanovich.

Addison, Joseph. 1992. On the Pleasures of the Imagination. Adams: 284–288.

Alcorn, Marshall W. 2002. *Changing the Subject in English Class: Discourse and the Construction of Desire*. Carbondale: Southern Illinois University Press.

Althusser, Louis. 1984. Ideology and Ideological State Apparatuses. In *Essays on Ideology*. London: Verso. 1–60.

Arieti, Silvano. 1976. *Creativity: The Magic Synthesis*. New York: Basic Books.

Aristotle. 1992. *Poetics*. Adams: 50–66.

Aristotle. 1991. *On Rhetoric: A Theory of Civic Discourse*. Trans. George A. Kennedy. Oxford: Oxford University Press.

Austin, John. 1962. *How to Do Things with Words*. Oxford: Oxford University Press.

Baecker, Diann L. 1998. Uncovering the Rhetoric of the Syllabus: The Case of the Missing *I*. *College Teaching* 46.2: 58–62.

Bain, Alexander. 1887. *English Composition and Rhetoric*. Enl. Ed. 2 vols. New York: American Book.

Bacon, Nora. 2000. Building a Swan's Nest for Instruction in Rhetoric. *College Composition and Communication* 51.4: 589–609.

Bakhtin, M.M. 1981. *The Dialogic Imagination*. Trans. Caryl Emerson and Michael Holquist. Ed. Michael Holquist. Austin: University of Texas Press.

Bakhtin, M.M. 1986. The Problem of Speech Genres. In *Speech Genres and Other Late Essays*. Eds. Caryl Emerson and Michael Holquist. Austin: University of Texas Press. 60–102.

Bartholomae, David. 1983. Writing Assignments: Where Writing Begins. In *Fforum: Essays on Theory and Practice in the Teaching of Writing*. Ed. Patricia L. Stock. Portsmouth: Boynton/Cook. 300–312.

Bartholomae, David. 1985. Inventing the University. In *When a Writer Can't Write.* Ed. Mike Rose. New York: Guilford. 134–65.

Bartholomae, David. 1995. Writing with Teachers: A Conversation with Peter Elbow. *College Composition and Communication* 46.1: 62–71.

Bawarshi, Anis, Amy J. Devitt, and Mary Jo Reiff. Forthcoming. Materiality and Genre in the Study of Discourse Community. *College English.*

Bazerman, Charles. 1988. *Shaping Written Knowledge: The Genre and Activity of the Experimental Article in Science.* Madison: University of Wisconsin Press.

Bazerman, Charles. 1994a. Systems of Genres and the Enactment of Social Intentions. Freedman and Medway (1994a): 79–101.

Bazerman, Charles. 1994b. Where is the Classroom? Freedman and Medway (1994b): 25–30

Bazerman, Charles. 1994c. Whose Moment? The Kairotics of Intersubjectivity. In *Constructing Experience.* Carbondale: Southern Illinois University Press. 171–193.

Bazerman, Charles. 1997a. Discursively Structured Activities. *Mind, Culture, and Activity* 4.4: 296–308.

Bazerman, Charles. 1997b. The Life of Genre, the Life in the Classroom. Bishop and Ostrom: 19–26.

Bazerman, Charles. 2000. A Rhetoric for Literate Society: The Tension between Expanding Practices and Restricted Theories. In *Inventing a Discipline: Rhetoric Scholarship in Honor of Richard E. Young.* Ed. Maureen Daly Goggin. Urbana: NCTE. 5–28.

Bazerman, Charles. 2002. Genre and Identity: Citizenship in the Age of the Internet and the Age of Global Capitalism. Coe, Lingard, and Teslenko: 13–37.

Bazerman, Charles, and James Paradis, Eds. 1991. *Textual Dynamics of the Professions: Historical and Contemporary Studies of Writing in Professional Communities.* Madison: University of Wisconsin Press.

Beaugrande, Robert Alain de. 1979. Toward a General Theory of Creativity. *Poetics* 8: 269–306.

Beebee, Thomas O. 1994. *The Ideology of Genre.* Pennsylvania: Pennsylvania State University Press.

Bergmann, Linda S. 1996. Academic Discourse and Academic Service: Composition vs. WAC in the University. *CEA Critic* 58.3: 50–59.

Berkenkotter, Carol. 2001. Genre Systems at Work: DSM IV and Rhetorical Recontextualization in Psychotherapy Paperwork. *Written Communication* 18.3: 326–349.

Berkenkotter, Carol, and Thomas N. Huckin. 1993. Rethinking Genre from a Sociocognitive Perspective. *Written Communication* 10.4: 475–509.

Berkenkotter, Carol, and Thomas N. Huckin. 1995. *Genre Knowledge in Disciplinary Communication: Cognition/Culture/Power.* Hillsdale: Lawrence Erlbaum.

Berlin, James. 1987. *Rhetoric and Reality: Writing Instruction in American Colleges, 1900–1985.* Carbondale: Southern Illinois University Press.

Berlin, James. 1996. *Rhetoric, Poetics, and Cultures: Refiguring College English Studies.* Urbana: NCTE.

Bhatia, Vijay K. 1993. *Analysing Genre: Language in Professional Settings.* London: Longman.

Bishop, Wendy. 1999. Places to Stand: The Reflective Writer–Teacher–Writer in Composition. *College Composition and Communication* 51.1: 9–31.

Bishop, Wendy and Hans Ostrom, Eds. 1997. *Genre and Writing: Issues, Arguments, Alternatives.* Portsmouth: Boynton/Cook.

Bitzer, Lloyd F. 1968. The Rhetorical Situation. *Philosophy and Rhetoric* 1: 1–14.

Bizzell, Patricia. 1992. *Academic Discourse and Critical Consciousness.* University of Pittsburgh Press.

Blair, Hugh. 1873. *Lectures on Rhetoric and Belles Lettres.* Philadelphia: Porter and Coates.

Blanchot, Maurice. 1959. *Le livre à venir.* Paris: Gallimard.

Bleich, David. 1988. *The Double Perspective: Language, Literacy, and Social Relations.* New York: Oxford University Press.

Booth, Wayne. 1974. *Modern Dogma and the Rhetoric of Assent.* Chicago: University of Chicago Press.

Bourdieu, Pierre. 1990. *The Logic of Practice.* Trans. Richard Nice. Stanford: Stanford University Press.

Bourdieu, Pierre. 1998. *On the Theory of Action.* Cambridge: Polity Press.

Branch, Kirk. 1998. From the Margins at the Center: Literacy, Authority, and the Great Divide. *College Composition and Communication* 30.2: 206–231.

Brereton, John C., Ed. 1995. *The Origins of Composition in the American College, 1875–1925: A Documentary History*. Pittsburgh: University of Pittsburgh Press.

Britton, James, et al. 1975. *The Development of Writing Abilities*. London: Macmillan.

Brodkey, Linda. 1987. *Academic Writing as Social Practice*. Philadelphia: Temple University Press.

Brooke, Robert. 1989. Control in Writing: Flower, Derrida, and Images of the Writer. *College English* 51.4: 405–417.

Brooke, Robert, and Dale Jacobs. 1997. Genre in Writing Workshops: Identity Negotiation and Student–Centered Writing. Bishop and Ostrom: 215–228.

Bruffee, Kenneth A. 1986. Social Construction, Language, and the Authority of Knowledge. *College English* 48: 773–790.

Burke, Kenneth. 1969a. *A Grammar of Motives*. Berkeley: University of California Press.

Burke, Kenneth. 1969b. *A Rhetoric of Motives*. Berkeley: University of California Press.

Campbell, Karlyn Kohrs. 1982. *The Rhetorical Act*. Blemont: Wadsworth.

Campbell, Karlyn Kohrs, and Kathleen M. Jamieson. 1978. *Form and Genre: Shaping Rhetorical Action*. Falls Church: Speech Communication Assoc.

Certeau, Michel de. 1984. *The Practice of Everyday Life*. Trans. Steven Rendall. Berkeley: University of California Press.

Christie, Frances. 1988. Genres as Choice. Reid: 22–34.

Christie, Frances. 1993. Curriculum Genres: Planning for Effective Teaching. Cope and Kalantzis: 154–178.

Christie, Frances, and J.R. Martin, Eds. 1997. *Genres and Institutions: Social Processes in the Workplace and School*. London: Cassell.

Clifford, John. 1991. The Subject in Discourse. In *Contending with Words*. Eds. Patricia Harkin and John Schilb. New York: MLA. 38–51.

Coe, Richard. 1994a. "An Arousing and Fulfilment of Desire": The Rhetoric of Genre in the Process Era and Beyond. Freedman and Medway (1994a): 181–186.

Coe, Richard. 1994b. Teaching Genre as Process. Freedman and Medway (1994b): 157–169.

Coe, Richard, Lorelei Lingard, and Tatiana Teslenko, Eds. 2002. *The Rhetoric and Ideology of Genre*. Cresskill, NJ: Hampton Press.

Cohen, Ralph. 1986. History and Genre. *New Literary History* 17.1: 203–218.

Cohen, Ralph. 1989. Do Postmodern Genres Exist? Perloff: 11–27.

Cohen, Ralph. 1991. Genre Theory, Literary History, and Historical Change. In *Theoretical Issues in Literary History*. Ed. David Perkins. Cambridge: Harvard University Press. 85–113.

Cole, M. and Y. Engeström. 1993. A Cultural–historical Approach to Distributed Cognition. In *Distributed Cognitions*. Ed. G. Salomon. Cambridge: Cambridge University Press. 1–46.

Cole, Thomas. 1991. *The Origins of Rhetoric in Ancient Greece*. Baltimore: Johns Hopkins University Press.

Connors, Robert J. 1981. The Rise and Fall of the Modes of Discourse. *College Composition and Communication* 32: 444–63.

Connors, Robert J. 1997. *Composition–Rhetoric: Backgrounds, Theory, and Pedagogy*. Pittsburgh: University of Pittsburgh Press.

Connors, Robert J., and Cheryl Glenn. 1995. *The St. Martin's Guide to Teaching Writing*. Third Edition. New York: St. Martin's Press.

Conrad, Joseph. 1988. *Heart of Darkness*. 3rd Ed. Ed. Robert Kimbrough. New York: W.W. Norton.

Consigny, Scott. 1994. Rhetoric and Its Situations. Young and Liu: 59–67.

Cooper, Marilyn. 1989. The Ecology of Writing. Cooper and Holzman: 1–12.

Cooper, Marilyn, and Michael Holzman. 1989. *Writing as Social Action*. New Hampshire: Boynton/Cook.

Cope, Bill, and Mary Kalantzis, eds. 1993. *The Powers of Literacy: A Genre Approach to Teaching Writing*. Pittsburgh: University of Pittsburgh Press.

Corbett, Edward P. J. 1990. *Classical Rhetoric for the Modern Reader* 3rd Ed. Oxford: Oxford University Press.

Corder, Jim. 1994. Varieties of Ethical Argument. Young and Liu: 99–133.

Croce, Benedetto. 1968. *Aesthetic*. Trans. Douglas Ainslie. New York: Noonday.

Crowley, Sharon. 1990. *The Methodical Memory: Invention in Current Traditional Rhetoric*. Southern Illinois University Press.

Crowley, Sharon. 1995. Composition's Ethic of Service, the Universal Requirement, and the Discourse of Student Need. *JAC: A Journal of Composition Theory* 15.2: 227–239.

Crowley, Sharon. 1998. *Composition in the University: Historical and Polemical Essays*. Pittsburgh: University of Pittsburgh Press.

Crowley, Sharon. 2000. Request for Opinions. WPA–L Discussion Group. WPA–L@ASU.EDU. August 28.

Culler, Jonathan. 1975. *Structuralist Poetics.* Ithaca: Cornell University Press.

D'Angelo, Frank. 1980. *Process and Thought in Composition.* 2nd. ed. Cambridge: Winthrope.

Dasenbrock, Reed Way. 1993. The Myths of the Subjective and of the Subject in Composition Studies. *JAC: A Journal of Composition Theory* 13.1: 21–32.

Derrida, Jacques. 1978. Freud and the Scene of Writing. In *Writing and Difference.* Trans. Alan Bass. Chicago: Chicago University Press. 196–231.

Derrida, Jacques. 1980. The Law of Genre. *Glyph* 7. Rpt. *Critical Inquiry* 7 (Autumn 1980): 55–81.

Derrida, Jacques. 1992. Structure, Sign and Play in the Discourse of the Human Sciences. Adams: 1117–1126.

Devitt, Amy J. 1991. Intertextuality in Tax Accounting: Generic, Referential, and Functional. Charles Bazerman and James Paradis: 335–357.

Devitt, Amy J. 1993. Generalizing about Genre: New Conceptions of an Old Concept. *College Composition and Communication* 44: 573–586.

Devitt, Amy J. 1997. Genre as Language Standard. Bishop and Ostrom: 45–55.

Dias, Patrick. 1994. Initiating Students into the Genres of Discipline–Based Reading and Writing. Freedman and Medway (1994b): 193–206.

Dubrow, Heather. 1982. *Genre.* London: Methune.

Ede, Lisa, and Andrea Lunsford. 1984. Audience Addressed/Audience Invoked: The Role of Audience in Composition Theory and Pedagogy. *College Composition and Communication* 35: 155–173.

Ede, Lisa, and Andrea Lunsford. 1990. *Singular Texts/ Plural Authors: Perspectives on Collaborative Writing.* Carbondale: Southern Illinois University Press.

Elbow, Peter. 1995. Being a Writer vs. Being an Academic: A Conflict in Goals. *College Composition and Communication* 46: 72–83.

Emig, Janet. 1964. The Uses of the Unconscious in Composing. *College Composition and Communication* 15: 6–11.

Emig, Janet. 1971. *The Composing Processes of Twelfth Graders*. Urbana: NCTE.

Enos, Theresa, Ed. 1996. *Encyclopedia of Rhetoric and Composition: Communication From Ancient Times to the Present*. New York: Garland.

Fahnestock, Jeanne. 1993. Genre and Rhetorical Craft. *Research in the Teaching of English* 27.3: 265–271.

Faigley, Lester. 1992. *Fragments of Rationality: Postmodernity and the Subject of Composition*. Pittsburgh: University of Pittsburgh Press.

Farrell, Thomas B. 1996. Commonplaces. Enos: 116–117.

Feldman, David Henry, Mihaly Csikszentmihalyi, and Howard Gardner. 1994. *Changing the World: A Framework for the Study of Creativity*. Westport: Praeger.

Fishelov, David. 1993. *Metaphors of Genre: The Role of Analogies in Genre Theory*. Pennsylvania: Penn. State University Press.

Flannery, Katherine T. 1991. Composing and the Question of Agency. *College English* 53: 701–713.

Fleming, David. 1998. Rhetoric as a Course of Study. *College English* 61.2: 169–191.

Flower, Linda S. 1994. *The Construction of Negotiated Meaning*. Carbondale: Southern Illinois University Press.

Flower, Linda S., and John R. Hays. 1980. The Cognition of Discovery: Defining a Rhetorical Problem. *College Composition and Communication* 31: 21–32.

Flower, Linda S., and John R. Hays. 1981. A Cognitive Process Theory of Writing. *College Composition and Communication* 32: 365–387.

Ford, Marjorie, and Jon Ford. 1998. *Dreams and Inward Journeys: A Rhetoric and Reader for Writers*. New York: Longman.

Foucault, Michel. 1994. What Is an Author? In *Contemporary Literary Criticism*. Third ed. Eds. Robert Con Davis and Ronald Schleifer. New York: Longman. 342–353.

Fowler, Alastair. 1982. *Kinds of Literature: An Introduction to the Theory of Genres and Modes*. Oxford: Oxford University Press.

Freadman, Anne. 1988. Anyone for Tennis? Reid: 91–124.

Freadman, Anne. 2002. Uptake. Coe, Lingard, and Teslenko: 39–53.

Freedman, Aviva. 1993a. Show and Tell? The Role of Explicit Teaching in the Learning of New Genres. *Research in the Teaching of English* 27: 222–251.

Freedman, Aviva. 1993b. Situating Genre: A Rejoinder. *Research in the Teaching of English* 27: 272–281.

Freedman, Aviva, and Peter Medway, Eds. 1994a. *Genre and the New Rhetoric*. Bristol: Taylor and Francis.

Freedman, Aviva, and Peter Medway, Eds. 1994b. *Learning and Teaching Genre*. Portsmouth: Boynton/Cook.

Freedman, Aviva, and Graham Smart. 1997. Navigating the Current of Economic Policy: Written Genres and the Distribution of Cognitive Work at a Financial Institution. *Mind, Culture, and Activity* 4.4: 238–255.

Frye, Northrop. 1957. *Anatomy of Criticism: Four Essays*. Princeton: Princeton University Press.

Fuller, Gillian, and Alison Lee. 2002. Assembling a Generic Subject. Coe, Lingard, and Teslenko: 207–224.

Geertz, Clifford. 1983. *Local Knowledge*. New York: Basic Books.

Genette, Gérard. 1992. *The Architext: An Introduction*. Berkeley: University of California Press.

Genung, John. 1887. The Study of Rhetoric in the College Course. Brereton: 133–157.

Genung, John. 1892. *The Practical Elements of Rhetoric*. Boston: Ginn.

Ghiselin, Brewster, ed. 1952. *The Creative Process*. Berkeley: University of California Press.

Giddens, Anthony. 1984. *The Constitution of Society: Outline of the Theory of Structuration*. Berkeley: University of California Press.

Giffen, Allison. 1997. Resisting Consolation: Early American Women Poets and the Elegiac Tradition. Bishop and Ostrom: 115–124.

Giltrow, Janet. 2002. Meta–Genre. Coe, Lingard, and Teslenko: 187–205.

Giltrow, Janet, and Michele Valiquette. 1994. Genres and Knowledge: Students Writing in the Disciplines. Freedman and Medway (1994b): 47–62.

Goffman, Erving. 1961. *Asylums: Essays on the Social Situation of Mental Patients and Other Inmates*. New York: Doubleday.

Graden, Sherrie L. 1995. *Romancing Rhetorics: Social Expressivist Perspectives on the Teaching of Writing*. Portsmouth: Boynton/Cook.

Green, Bill, and Alison Lee. 1994. Writing Geography: Literacy, Identity, and Schooling. Freedman and Medway (1994b): 207–224.

Greenblatt, Stephen. 1982. Introduction to Special Issue on the Forms of Power and the Power of Forms in the Renaissance. *Genre* 15.1,2: 3–6.

Hart, John S. 1877. *A Manual of Composition and Rhetoric: A Textbook for Schools and Colleges*. Philadelphia: Eldredge.

Halasek, Kay. 1999. *A Pedagogy of Possibility: Bakhtinian Perspectives on Composition Studies*. Carbondale: Southern Illinois University Press.

Halliday, M.A.K. 1978. *Language as Social Semiotic: The Social Interpretation of Language and Meaning*. London: Edward Arnold.

Harris, Joseph. 1997. *A Teaching Subject: Composition Since 1966*. New Jersey: Prentice Hall.

Hatch, Gary Layne. 1999. *Arguing in Communities*. 2nd Edition. Mountain View, CA: Mayfield.

Hausman, Carl R. 1984. *A Discourse on Novelty and Creation*. Albany: State University of New York Press.

Heidegger, Martin. 1992. Building, Dwelling, Thinking. In *The Metaphysical Foundations of Logic*. Trans. Michael Heim. Bloomington: Indiana University Press.

Heilker, Paul. 1997. Rhetoric Made Real: Civil Discourse and Writing Beyond the Curriculum. In *Writing the Community*. Ed. Linda Adler–Kassner, Robert Crooks, and Ann Watters. Washington D.C.: American Association for Higher Education. 71–76.

Helscher, Thomas P. 1997. The Subject of Genre. Bishop and Ostrom: 27–36.

Hill, Adams Sherman. 1878. *The Principles of Rhetoric and Their Amplification*. Rev. enl. ed. New York: American Book.

Hill, Charles A., and Lauren Resnick. 1995. Creating Opportunities for Apprenticeship in Writing. In *Reconceiving Writing, Rethinking Writing Instruction*. Ed. Joseph Petraglia. Mahwah: Lawrence Erlbaum.

Hirsch, E.D. 1967. *Validity in Interpretation*. New Haven: Yale University Press.

Howard, Rebecca Moore. 1999. *Standing in the Shadow of Giants: Plagiarists, Authors, and Collaborators*. Stamford: Ablex.

Jameson, Fredric. 1981. *The Political Unconscious: Narrative as a Socially Symbolic Act*. Ithaca: Cornell University Press.

Jamieson, Kathleen M. 1973. Generic Constraints and the Rhetorical Situation. *Philosophy and Rhetoric* 6: 163.

Jamieson, Kathleen M. 1975. Antecedent Genre as Rhetorical Constraint. *Quarterly Journal of Speech* 61: 406–15.

Jarratt, Susan C. 1991. *Rereading the Sophists: Classical Rhetoric Refigured.* Carbondale: Southern Illinois University Press.

Kant, Immanuel. 1992. From *Critique of Judgement.* Adams: 376–393.

Kent, Thomas. 1991. On the Very Idea of a Discourse Community. *College Composition and Communication* 42: 425–445.

Kent, Thomas, Ed. 1999. *Post–Process Theory: Beyond the Writing–Process Paradigm.* Carbondale: Southern Illinois University Press.

Knoblauch, C.H., and Lil Brannon. 1984. *Rhetorical Traditions and the Teaching of Writing.* New Hampshire: Boynton/Cook.

Kress, Gunther. 1988. Genre in a Social Theory of Language: A Reply to John Dixon. Reid: 35–45.

Kress, Gunther. 1993. Genre as Social Process. Cope and Kalantzis: 22–37.

Kuhn, Thomas. 1970. *The Structure of Scientific Revolution.* Chicago: University of Chicago Press.

Lakoff, George, and Mark Johnson. 1980. *Metaphors We Live By.* Chicago: University of Chicago Press.

Lawrence, D.H. 1977. *Sons and Lovers: Text, Background, and Criticism.* Ed. Julian Moynahan. New York: Penguin.

Lauer, Janice M. 1967. Invention in Contemporary Rhetoric: Heuristic Procedures. Unpublished Doctoral Dissertation. University of Michigan.

Lauer, Janice M. 1970. Heuristics and Composition. In *Contemporary Rhetoric: A Conceptual Background with Readings.* Ed. Ross Winterowd. NY: Harcourt: 79–90.

Lauer, Janice M. 1984. Issues in Rhetorical Invention. In *Essays on Classical Rhetoric and Modern Discourse.* Eds. Robert Connors, Lisa Ede, and Andrea Lunsford. Carbondale: Southern Illinois University Press. 127–139.

Lauer, Janice M. 1996. Topics. Enos: 724–725.

LeFevre, Karen Burke. 1987. *Invention as a Social Act.* Carbondale: Southern Illinois University Press.

Lindemann, Erika. 1995. *A Rhetoric for Writing Teachers.* 3rd. ed. New York: Oxford University Press.

Locke, John. 1992. From *Essay Concerning Human Understanding.* Adams: 254–268.

Lovitt, Carl R., and Art Young. 1997. Rethinking Genre in the First–Year Composition Course: Helping Student Writers Get Things Done. *Profession 1997*: 113–125.

Lu, Min–zhan. 1991. Redefining the Legacy of Mina Shaughnessy: A Critique of the Politics of Linguistic Innocence. *Journal of Basic Writing* 10.1: 26–40.

Lunsford, Andrea A., and Lisa Ede. 1994. Collaborative Authorship and the Teaching of Writing. Woodmansee and Jaszi: 418–438.

Maimon, Elaine. 1983. Maps and Genres: Exploring Connections in the Arts and Sciences. In *Composition and Literature: Bridging the Gap*. Ed. Winifred Bryan Horner. Chicago: University of Chicago Press. 110–125.

Martin, J.R. 1992. *English Text: System and Structure*. Amsterdam: Benjamins.

Martin, J.R. 1997. Analyzing Genre: Functional Parameters. Christie and Martin: 33–69.

Medway, Peter. 1998. Understanding Architects' Notebooks: Does Genre Theory Help? Symposium on Genre: Literacy and Literature. Simon Fraser University, January.

Medway, Peter. 2002. Fuzzy Genres and Community Identity: The Case of Architecture Students' Sketchbooks. Coe, Lingard, and Teslenko: 123–153.

Miller, Carolyn R. 1979. A Humanistic Rationale for Technical Writing. *College English* 40.6: 610–617.

Miller, Carolyn R. 1980. Vocationalism and Vision in Writing Courses. *JGE: The Journal of General Education* 32.3: 239–246.

Miller, Carolyn R. 1984. Genre as Social Action. *Quarterly Journal of Speech* 70: 151–167.

Miller, Carolyn R. 1992. Kairos in the Rhetoric of Science. In *A Rhetoric of Doing*. Eds. S.P. Witte, N. Nakadato, and R.D. Cherry. Carbondale: Southern Illinois University Press. 310–327.

Miller, Carolyn R. 1994. Rhetorical Community: The Cultural Basis of Genre. Freedman and Medway (1994a): 67–77.

Miller, Carolyn R. 1999. On the Borders between Disciplines: An Interview with Carolyn Miller. By Mary Jo Reiff and Anis Bawarshi. *Issues in Writing* 9.2: 110–138.

Miller, Susan. 1989. *Rescuing the Subject: A Critical Introduction to Rhetoric and the Writer*. Carbondale: Southern Illinois University Press.

Miller, Susan. 1991. *Textual Carnivals: The Politics of Composition*. Carbondale: Southern Illinois University Press.

Miller, Susan. 1997. Technologies of Self?–Formation. *JAC: A Journal of Composition Theory* 17.3: 497–500.

Miller, Thomas P. 1997. *The Formation of College English: Rhetoric and Belles Lettres in the British Cultural Provinces*. Pittsburgh: University of Pittsburgh Press.

Mühlhäusler, P., and R. Harré. 1990. *Pronouns and People: The Linguistic Construction of Social and Personal Identity*. Oxford: Basil and Blackwell.

Munby, J. 1978. *Communicative Syllabus Design*. Cambridge: Cambridge University Press.

Murphy, James J, Ed. 1990. *A Short History of Writing Instruction From Ancient Greece to Twentieth–Century America*. Davis: Hermagoras Press.

Murray, Donald. 1989. *Expecting the Unexpected: Teaching Myself and Others to Read and Write*. Portsmouth: Boynton/Cook.

Newman, Samuel. 1838. *A Practical System of Rhetoric or The Principles and Rules of Style Inferred from Examples of Writing, to Which is Added a Historical Dissertation on English Style*. 7th. Ed. Boston: Newman.

Ohmann, Richard. 1976. *English in America*. New York: Oxford University Press.

Paré, Anthony. 1998. Professional Persona: Erasing the Self from Official Stories. Conference on College Composition and Communication. Chicago. April 2.

Paré, Anthony. 2002. Genre and Identity: Individuals, Institutions, and Ideology. Coe, Lingrad, and Teslenko: 57–71.

Paré, Anthony, and Graham Smart. 1994. Observing Genres in Action: Towards a Research Methodology. Freedman and Medway (1994a): 146–154.

Pelkowski, Stephanie. 1998. The Teacher's Audience is Always a Fiction. Unpublished Manuscript.

Perelman, C.H. 1982. *The Realm of Rhetoric*. Trans. William Kluback. Notre Dame: University of Notre Dame Press.

Perelman, C.H., and L. Olbrechts–Tyteca. 1969. *The New Rhetoric: A Treatise on Argumentation*. Trans. John Wilkinson and Purcell Weaver. Notre Dame: University of Notre Dame Press.

Perkins, David. 1981. *The Mind's Best Work*. Cambridge: Harvard University Press.

Perl, Sondra. 1979. The Composing Processes of Unskilled College Writers. *Research in the Teaching of English* 13: 317–336.

Perl, Sondra. 1988. Understanding Composing. In *The Writing Teacher's Sourcebook*. Eds. Gary Tate and Edward P.J. Corbett. Oxford: Oxford University Press. 113–118.

Perloff, Marjorie, ed. 1989. *Postmodern Genres*. Norman: University of Oklahoma Press.

Peters, Brad. 1997. Genre, Antigenre, and Reinventing the Forms of Conceptualization. Bishop and Ostrom: 199–214.

Petruzzi, Anthony. 1998. Between Conventions and Critical Thinking: The Concept of "Limit–Situations" in Critical Literacy and Pedagogy. *JAC: A Journal of Composition Theory* 18.2: 310–332.

Pfau, Thomas. 1994. The Pragmatics of Genre: Moral Theory and Lyric Authorship in Hegel and Wordsworth. Woodmansee and Jaszi: 138–158.

Popken, Randall. 1999. The Pedagogical Dissemination of a Genre: The Resume in American Business Discourse Textbooks, 1914–1939. *JAC: A Journal of Composition Theory* 19.1: 91–116.

Reid, Ian, Ed. 1988. *The Place of Genre in Learning: Current Debates*. Geelong: Deakin University.

Reiff, John D., and James E. Middleton. 1983. A Model for Designing and Revising Assignments. Stock: 263–268.

Reynolds, Nedra. 1998. Composition's Imagined Geographies: The Politics of Space in the Frontier, City, and Cyberspace. *College Composition and Communication* 50.1: 12–35.

Richards, I.A. 1936. *The Philosophy of Rhetoric*. Oxford: Oxford University Press.

Rohman, D. Gordon. 1994. Pre–Writing: The Stage of Discovery in the Writing Process. Young and Liu: 41–49.

Rose, Mark. 1993. *Authors and Owners: The Invention of Copyright*. Cambridge: Harvard University Press.

Rose, Nikolas. 1996. *Inventing Ourselves: Psychology, Power, and Personhood*. Cambridge: Cambridge University Press.

Rosmarin, Adena. 1985. *The Power of Genre*. Minneapolis: University of Minnesota Press.

Rothenberg, Albert. 1979. *The Emerging Goddess*. Chicago: University of Chicago Press.

Russell, David. 1991. *Writing in the Academic Disciplines, 1870–1990: A Curricular History*. Carbondale: Southern Illinois University Press.

Russell, David R. 1997. Rethinking Genre in School and Society: An Activity Theory Analysis. *Written Communication* 14.4: 504–554.

Russell, David R. 2002. The Kind–ness of Genre: An Activity Theory Analysis of High School Teachers' Perceptions of Genre in Portfolio Assessment Across the Curriculum. Coe, Lingard, and Teslenko: 225–242.

Sacks, Peter M. 1985. *The English Elegy: Studies in the Genre from Spenser to Yates*. Baltimore: Johns Hopkins University Press.

Said, Edward. 1975. *Beginnings: Intention and Method*. New York: Columbia University Press.

de Saussure, Ferdinand. 1966. *Course in General Linguistics*. Trans. Wade Baskin. New York: McGraw–Hill.

Schell, Eileen. 1997. Response to Wendy Hesford. Bishop and Ostrom: 172–175.

Scholes, Robert E. 1975. *Structuralism in Literature: An Introduction*. New Haven: Yale University Press.

Schreiner, Steven. 1997. A Portrait of the Student as a Young Writer: Re–evaluating Emig and the Process Movement. *College Composition and Communication* 48.1: 86–104.

Schryer, Catherine F. 1994. The Lab vs. the Clinic: Sites of Competing Genres. Freedman and Medway (1994a): 105–124.

Schryer, Catherine F. 1999. Genre Time/Space: Chronotopic Strategies in the Experimental Article. *JAC: A Journal of Composition Theory* 19.1: 81–89.

Schryer, Catherine F. 2002. Genre and Power: A Chronotopic Analysis. Coe, Lingard, and Teslenko: 73–102.

Scott, Fred Newton, and Joseph Villiers Denney. 1902. *Composition–Literature*. Boston: Allyn.

Searle, John. 1969. *Speech Acts: An Essay in the Philosophy of Language*. Cambridge: Cambridge University Press.

Slevin, James F. 1988. Genre Theory, Academic Discourse, and Writing in the Disciplines. In *Audits of Meaning: A Festschrift in*

*Honor of Anne E. Berthoff*. Ed. Louise Z. Smith. Portsmouth: Boynton Cook. 3–16.

Smith, Frank. 1994. *Understanding Reading*. 5th Ed. Hillsdale: Lawrence Erlbaum.

Sommers, Nancy. 1982. Responding to Student Writing. *College Composition and Communication* 33.2: 148–156.

Spellmeyer, Kurt. 1989. Foucault and the Freshman Writer: Considering the Self in Discourse. *College English* 51: 715–729.

Spivak, Gayatri. 1976. Translator's Preface. In *Of Grammatology*, Jacques Derrida. Baltimore: Johns Hopkins University Press. ix–lxxxvii.

Stock, Patricia L., Ed. 1983. *Fforum: Essays on Theory and Practice in the Teaching of Writing*. Portsmouth: Boynton/Cook.

Stygall, Gail. 1994. Resisting Privilege: Basic Writing and Foucault's Author Function. *College Composition and Communication* 45: 320–341.

Swales, John M. 1990. *Genre Analysis: English in Academic and Research Settings*. Cambridge: Cambridge University Press.

Swales, John M. 1996. Occluded Genres in the Academy: The Case of the Submission Letter. In *Academic Writing: Intercultural and Textual Issues*. Amsterdam: John Benjamins Publishing. 44–58.

Swales, John M. 1998. *Other Floors, Other Voices: A Textography of a Small University Building*. Mahway, NJ: Lawrence Erlbaum.

Threadgold, Terry. 1989. Talking about Genre: Ideologies and Incompatible Discourses. *Cultural Studies* 3.1: 101–27.

Trimbur, John. 2002. *Call to Write*. 2nd Edition. New York: Longman.

Todorov, Tzvetan. 1970. *The Fantastic: A Structural Approach to a Literary Genre*. Trans. Richard Howard. Ithaca: Cornell University Press.

Todorov, Tzvetan. 1976. The Origin of Genres. *New Literary History* 8.1: 159–170.

Tran, Teresa. 1997. A Patient as an Object. Unpublished Manuscript.

Villanueva, Victor. 1993. *Bootstraps: From an American Academic of Color*. Urbana: NCTE.

Vitanza, Victor J. 1999. "The Wasteland Grows"; Or, What is "Cultural Studies for Composition" and Why Must We Always Speak Good of It?: ParaResponse to Julie Drew. *JAC: A Journal of Composition Theory* 19.4: 699–703.

Vygotsky, Lev. 1986. *Thought and Language*. Cambridge: MIT Press.

Watt, Ian. 1983. *The Rise of the Novel.* Berkeley: University of California Press.

Weisberg, Robert. 1993. *Creativity: Beyond the Myth of Genius.* New York: W.H. Freeman.

Wellek, René, and Austin Warren. 1942. *Theory of Literature.* New York: Harvest.

Williams, James D. 1989. *Preparing to Teach Writing.* Belmont: Wadsworth.

Williams, Joseph M., and Gregory G. Colomb. 1993. The Case for Explicit Teaching: Why What You Don't Know Won't Help You. *Research in the Teaching of English* 27.3: 252–264.

Williams, Patricia J. 1992. *The Alchemy of Race and Rights.* Cambridge: Harvard University Press.

Williams, Raymond. 1981. *Problems in Materialism and Culture.* New York: Schocken.

Woodman, Leonora, and Thomas P. Adler. 1988. *The Writer's Choices with Handbook.* 2nd. Ed. Glenview, IL: Scott.

Woodmansee, Martha, and Peter Jaszi, eds. 1994. *The Construction of the Author: Textual Appropriation in Law and Literature.* Durham: Duke University Press.

Worsham, Lynn. 1991. Writing Against Writing: The Predicament of Ècriture Féminine. In *Contending with Words: Composition and Rhetoric in a Postmodern Age.* Eds. Patricia Harkin and John Schilb. NY: MLA.

Yates, JoAnne. 1989. *Control Through Communication: The Rise of System in American Management.* Baltimore: Johns Hopkins University Press.

Yates, JoAnne, and Wanda Orlikowski. 1992. Genres of Organizational Communication: A Structural Approach. *Academy of Management Review* 17: 299–326.

Yates, JoAnne, and Wanda Orlikowski. 2002. Genres Systems: Chronos and Kairos in Communicative Interaction. Coe, Lingard, and Teslenko: 103–121.

Young, Edward. 1992. From *Conjectures on Original Composition.* Adams: 329–337.

Young, Richard. 1978. Paradigms and Problems: Needed Research in Rhetorical Invention. In *Research on Composing: Points of Departure.* Eds. Charles R. Cooper and Lee Odell. Urbana: NCTE. 29–47.

Young, Richard. 1986. Invention: A Topographical Survey. In *Teaching Composition: Twelve Bibliographic Essays.* Ed. Gary Tate. Fort Worth: Texas Christian University Press. 1–43.

Young, Richard. 1994. Concepts of Art and the Teaching of Writing. Young and Liu: 193–202.

Young, Richard, Alton Becker, and Kenneth Pike. 1970. *Rhetoric: Discovery and Change.* NY: Harcourt.

Young, Richard, and Yameng Liu, Eds. 1994. *Landmark Essays on Rhetorical Invention.* Davis: Hermagoras Press.

# INDEX

ANIS BAWARSHI is assistant professor of English at the University of Washington, where he teaches courses in composition theory and pedagogy, genre theory, discourse analysis, and language policy. He has recently co-edited (with Sidney I. Dobrin) a composition reader, *A Closer Look: A Writer's Reader* (McGraw Hill) and is currently co-authoring (with Amy J. Devitt and Mary Jo Reiff) a composition textbook that uses genres to help students write in different scenes of writing, *Scenes of Writing: Genre Acts* (Longman). His articles and scholarly interviews have appeared in *Ecocomposition: Theoretical and Pedagogical Approaches* (an edited collection), *College English, JAC: A Journal of Composition Theory, The Writing Center Journal, Issues in Writing, Composition Forum,* and *Writing on the Edge.*